Game-Changing Christianity

How the early Christians so radically influenced their world and what we can learn from them.

Dwight Edwards

Printed in the United States of America

First Printing, 2016

ISBN: 978-1-5356-0119-1

Praise for Game-Changing Christianity

"King Solomon said 'There is nothing new under the sun'. In the same manner, Dwight has tapped into time honored but often forgotten principles for how we should integrate our faith into our work and lives. *Game-Changing Christianity* is a must read."

__**Greg Brenneman**, former president of Continental Airline, CEO of Quiznos Sub, former CEO of Burger King, CEO of CCMP, and author of *Right Way & All At Once*

"With roughly 25% of Americans describing themselves as evangelical, why is the number of people calling themselves Christians steadily declining? Dwight Edwards digs deeply into the key components and attributes of evangelism as it existed in the early church. Why did Christianity spread so fast, so far? Dwight's examination of scripture, especially his insights into the books of Thessalonians, and his judicious use of quotations from some of history's greatest evangelists, result in a compelling argument for a change. His latest effort is a superb, tightly crafted work defining game-changing Christianity. A game changer for evangelism it should be. It was a game changer for me personally. And changed you will be upon reading Dwight's *Game-Changing Christianity*."

__**Lloyd Bentsen**, Founding Chairman of National Christian Foundation Houston , Chairman of the Investment

Committee of National Christian Foundation, and serves on the board of the Barnabas Group

"Both the method and content of Dwight's latest inspired and inspirational writing, has brought life-challenging and life-changing revelation to my heart and mind. *Game-Changing Christianity* has truly been a game changer for me personally. It had never occurred to me that those first century believers could impact me so deeply and personally. I know that this book will change all who read it, savoring all it contains, as it intrigues, captures, and gives us no option than to digest and allow it to nourish our inner beings. As an avid reader, learner, teacher and counsellor, I cannot recommend this book more highly to all, no matter who you are. (Go ahead, take the first bite; you will immediately understand what I mean!)"

__**Jenny Lowen**, veteran missionary with YWAM in England

"Dwight Edwards, *Game-Changing Christianity*, is a fresh reminder calling the church to embrace the biblical reason for its existence. His creative interweaving of Scripture, early church history and striking quotes not only underscore the basics of faith, hope and love but pinpoint strategic principles from the past which are key in penetrating the contemporary world for our Lord and Savior."

__**Dr. Walt Baker**, longtime missionary to Haiti and associate professor emeritus of world missions at Dallas Theological Seminary

"This book dares us to live a dangerous Christianity --- one that will make a difference now and for eternity. One of the key game changing truths Edwards brings out so powerfully is that too often our greatest passion is for a CAUSE rather than for a PERSON.

Every pastor, indeed, every serious Christian should read this book to quicken their walk and capture the urgency of the Gospel.......a book for any Christian to catch fire for God or any pastor looking for the keys to spiritual growth for himself and his congregation. This book contains one simple truth and reminder after another of the way the early converts lived life and did ministry. What lessons for us 'modern, sophisticated' believers!"

__**Bob Doll**, Chief Equity Strategist and Senior Portfolio Manager at Nuveen Asset Management. He also serves as a board member of National Christian Foundation, Kingdom Advisors, and New Canaan Society.

"Dwight is a great writer in combining history and theology. He reminds us how the early church was started, about the passion of the first saints, and how the same game plan should still be applied today. Each of us is called to spread the Word in our own circles of influence. We are all in ministry. Dwight illustrates this clearly in the movement of the first believers."

__**Jim Smith**, president of Smithco Development and board member of Star of Hope, Young Life, HBU, and other organizations

"I've had the privilege to know Dwight Edwards for many years, and I'm constantly amazed at his insights. His new book,

Game-Changing Christianity, is the wakeup call Christians desperately need. It takes us back to the roots of the vibrant, thrilling, first-century church, and it reminds us that real faith is a life of surprise and adventure. If you read only one book this year, this should be it!"

__**Laura Seifert**, founder of *Yes. Ministries* and highly sought bible teacher

"Encouraging, convicting, motivating, Game-Changing Christianity moves us all out of comfort zones and into an exciting place where the Lord can use any and all of us to impact the kingdom. The book offers a kind but firm nudge to help us understand that the world is always longing to hear the Good News and we are the ones to bring it. Let's all commit being game-changers for our generation, for His glory."

__**Courtney Garrett**, Director & blog contributor for *Sacred Story Ministries*, Dallas Theological Seminary graduate, women's discipleship leader and gifted communicator.

Dedication

This book is dedicated to *WatersEdge Community Church*. What a privilege it is to open God's word each week to such amazing saints! You have helped me to believe that what I have written regarding the early Christians could actually happen again today. Thank you!

Contents

Foreword

WHEN THE GAME CHANGES, EXCITEMENT ensues! The buzzer beater, the hail Mary pass, or the innovation that society can't seem to live without are all game changers. Far more important than the excitement of an impact sport or the latest in technology is the game changing of a soul. When we are radically changed it becomes contagious. It spreads. Rarely does a change in a player morph the entire sport, but the heart of a Christian can transform the entirety of history. The first generation of believers revolutionized their world. Wildfire, passion, sweeping impact...game changing can all be used to express the difference they made. Low on resources but high in prayer, they altered the world. Is it possible for us to see God use today's saints in similar ways? Is He still in the business of molding the hearts He created to glorify Him? A resounding yes! This book will inspire you that not only can He, but He wants to. And most importantly, He can take any available man or woman and turn them into game changers. Game changers who are targeting the soul not just the scoreboard.

Dwight Edwards has been a part of my life as a game changer for decades. If I were to list the top five spiritual influencers in my life, he would be there. As my pastor during college and my friend during adulthood, I've seen his scholarship, brilliance, and wisdom impact thousands of hearts including mine. "Game

Changing Christianity" will ignite a passion in you to live more for the things of God than the things of this world.

We all want to make a difference but often lack the inspiration and instruction on how to. Allow these pages to inspire your heart and structure your steps as the Holy Spirit does his work in and through you. As in the early church, when God is involved in the world, Game Changers will be called out…be one of them! This book will help you like few others.

Gregg Matte - Founder of Breakaway Ministries, senior pastor of Houston's First Baptist Church, and author of *Unstoppable Gospel*

Introduction

"Truths...are too often considered as so true that they lose all the powers of truth, and lie bed-ridden in the dormitory of the soul, side by side with the most despised and exploded errors." Samuel Taylor Coleridge

Nobody disputes it. The first 300 years of Christianity were epic years. They were the legendary years of unparalleled gospel penetration. In them we find the storied days of the church's radical, wholesale participation in spreading the gospel's stunningly good news far and wide. By only the year 150 A.D., Justin Martyr would write, "*For there is not one single race of men, whether barbarians, or Greeks, or whatever they may be called, nomads, or vagrants, or herdsmen living in tents, among whom prayers and giving of thanks are not offered through the name of the crucified Jesus.*" In barely more than a century, an unpromising band of 120 men and women had multiplied so rapidly that their message had infiltrated practically every nook and cranny of their known world.

Dr. Rodney Stark, a Princeton sociologist, has written a fascinating work entitled "The Rise of Christianity: *How the Obscure, Marginal Jesus Movement Became the Dominant Religious Force in the Western World.*" In it he provides the following research estimates concerning the numerical growth of Christians in the first 300 years of the church:

Year	Number of Christians	Percentage of Population
100	7,530	.0126

150	40,496	.07
200	217,795	.36
250	1,171,356	1.9
300	6,299,832	10.5
350	33,882,008	56.0

Amazing, isn't it? In just around 300 years, the ripples of these earliest believers' lives had launched a spiritual tsunami throughout the Roman Empire. And the question has to be asked—what was the secret behind such success?

If these saints of the first 300 years could come back and offer us a word of advice for furthering the good news in our day, what would they say? What formula would they let us in on? What long kept secret would they reveal? I truly, truly believe they would plead:

"Go back to the original game plan. Go back and rediscover the reasons why it was said of us, 'These who have turned the world upside down have come here also.' Go back and study afresh the values, strategies, and practices for dynamic gospel penetration as laid down in the New Testament. Especially focus on the teachings our greatest game changer other than Jesus—Paul. Go back, go back, go back! The game plan has always been there; it just hasn't been utilized outside the first 300 years of Christendom well enough or often enough. But it is powerful! So, so powerful! It worked for us, it has worked for others after us, and it will work for you, if you will just give it the chance. There's absolutely no reason you couldn't join us as significant game changers in the people's lives of your day. Eternal game changers."

Now, going back doesn't mean that I believe the early church was perfect. No, not by a long shot. Even a cursory reading of the epistles of the New Testament reveals a Christian community pockmarked in varying degrees by carnality, legalism, false teaching, divisions, hypocrisy, and more. Yet somehow—with no printing press, no church buildings, no seminaries, no radio or television, no mass mailings, no Internet, no Christian concerts, no church growth experts, and most of all, no clergy—these Christ-followers remain unrivaled in the "gospeling" of the world in their day. **In fact, the stunning historical reality is this–Christianity was at its best when it had no clergy and no church buildings!** But how could this be? I think the reason is both profoundly simple and profoundly powerful. Like great athletes, they simply did the basics extraordinarily, tirelessly, and relentlessly well.

What then were these basics? The rest of this book will be devoted to identifying and exploring them. But because these fundamentals are so basic and familiar, we run the danger described by Coleridge, *"Truths...are too often considered as so true that they lose all the powers of truth, and lie bed-ridden in the dormitory of the soul, side by side with the most despised and exploded errors."* In other words, truths which become overly familiar to us run the risk of having no more practical effect on our lives than the errors we reject. We become numb to them and internally yawn when they are presented. But just because something is basic, just because something is exceedingly familiar, just because something no longer jars us, it doesn't mean that that something isn't exceedingly, extraordinarily potent.

It's time that these basic but oh-so-powerful truths no longer remain bedridden in the dormitory of our souls. It's time that they take up their bed to walk once again. I invite you then, my friend, to come back with me in time to dust off those basics and rediscover their astonishing game-changing power for today.

Chapter 1

THE CALL TO DANGEROUS CHRISTIANITY

"We are so utterly ordinary, so commonplace, while we profess to know a Power the Twentieth Century does not reckon with. But we are 'harmless,' and therefore unharmed. We are spiritual pacifists, non-militants, conscientious objectors in this battle-to-the-death with principalities and powers in high places. We are 'sideliners' coaching and criticizing the real wrestlers while content to sit by and leave the enemies of God unchallenged. The world cannot hate us, we are too much like its own. Oh that God would make us dangerous!"
—Jim Elliot

DANGEROUS CHRISTIANITY. WHAT STIRS WITHIN you, if anything, when you read this phrase? My guess is that some of you find yourselves intrigued by it, perhaps even excited to see what lies ahead in this book. Others of you are puzzled, wondering how the words *dangerous* and *Christianity* could ever go together. And still others of you find yourselves somewhat recoiling at the phrase, for it reminds you of the all too many reckless, destructive actions carried out by misguided believers in the name of God. Trust me, I hear you.

There have been way too many times in the history of the church when Christianity has been dangerous in all the wrong ways. The Crusades, the Spanish Inquisition, burning heretics at the stake, the Salem witch trials, etc., all serve as monstrously black eyes on the face of Christendom. More recently, bombing abortion clinics and attacking gays remind us that some forms of Christianity can still be dangerous in the worst of ways.

But in spite of all its abuses, the church cannot escape its calling to be dangerous. Dangerous in the right ways...for the right reasons...at the right times. It is a grace-soaked kind of danger, a Christ-scented militancy, a Spirit-empowered blitzkrieg into enemy territory. The true enemy, that is. It is a revolution of unexpected kindness, surprising mercy, breath-taking humility, and relentless spotlighting our King. And in the end, it is the most dangerous danger known to men and angels.

There are many, many places we could go in the scripture to find a mandate to be dangerous. For the moment, I will limit myself to two key passages. The first is found in the sixteenth chapter of Matthew.

"Jesus answered and said to him, 'Blessed are you, Simon Bar-Jonah, for flesh and blood has not revealed this to you, but My Father who is in heaven. And I also say to you that you are Peter, and on this rock I will build My church, and the gates of Hades shall not prevail against it.'" (Mtt. 16:17,18)

I am totally intrigued with this passage. First of all, it is the very first mention of the "*church*" in the New Testament. The word for church—ekklesia—most literally means "*called out ones.*" The church is simply the aggregate sum of the "*called out*" flesh and blood believers. This word has absolutely nothing to do with buildings, organizations, programs, etc. It has everything, but everything, to do with people. Frail, fallen, stick-'em-and-they-bleed people like you and me. People purchased by the precious blood of Christ. People indwelt by the fiery Spirit of God. People called *out* from spiritual darkness and eternal death. But what, in God's name, are we called *to*?

How fascinating that the very first purpose Christ mentions for His "called out ones" is militant. We are essentially going to be transformed into a battering ram. A Christ-constructed and a Christ-empowered battering ram. "*…I will build My church, and the gates of Hades shall not prevail against it.*" Or to put it another way, we are here to be gate crashers. Our Lord is gathering an army of men, women, boys, and girls who will march headlong into enemy strongholds ("*gates*") and find these gates giving way to that Name above all names. Ordinary, struggling, run of the mill, mostly unheralded people like you and me are going to serve in a cosmic war that should really only be fought by angels. We have received our marching orders to be part of a shock and awe campaign directed at hell itself. What an amazing calling! What a lofty privilege! What a high adventure! And yes, what a dangerous job assignment.

Christ could easily have said, "I will build My church, and great worship will arise from it." Or, "I will build My church, and societies will be powerfully blessed by it." Or still yet, "I will build My church, and it will become a refuge from a hostile world." These things are true and most certainly have their place in church life**. But we cannot blink the fact that the first job description Christ gave to the church was storming the gates of hell itself**, for us to be divinely empowered gate crashers.

Certainly the church has other functions than warfare. Important functions, godly functions, not-to-be-neglected functions. **And let me hasten to say that our first and highest calling is not war. It is love.** *"Jesus said to him, 'You shall love the Lord your God with all your heart, with all your soul, and with all your mind.' This is the first and great commandment. And the second is like it: 'You shall love your neighbor as yourself,'"* (Mtt. 22:37-39.) Our greatest calling in life is the cultivating of a white-hot, ever-deepening love affair with our God and the releasing of God-tainted love towards those around us. Both saved and unsaved. Nothing rivals the supremacy and importance of this love calling. Yet according to our Lord, we are here for more than love. His "called out ones" are in a ceaseless, truce-less, cosmic conflict against the very powers of hell itself. "*The church*", as one writer put it, "*is born for battle.*" We dare not settle for anything less.

Our second passage is found in the sixth chapter of Ephesians.

"Finally, my brethren, be strong in the Lord and in the power of His might. Put on the whole armor of God, that you may be able to stand against the wiles of the devil. For we do not wrestle against flesh and blood, but against principalities, against powers, against the rulers of the darkness of this age, against spiritual hosts of wickedness in the heavenly places. Therefore take up the whole armor of God, that you may be able to withstand in the evil day, and having done all, to stand," (Eph. 6:10-13.)

Again, this is such a crucial passage, particularly in light of its context within the book of Ephesians. The letter to the

Ephesians is one of only two non-corrective epistles by Paul in the New Testament. In other words, almost all his epistles are written to help correct a problem or address an issue. Galatians is written to ward off legalism, I Corinthians to deal with carnality, etc. But only Romans and Ephesians are written to expound the Christian life from beginning to end. Each epistle is carefully sequenced; with each section purposefully building upon the previous section. What this means is that the *order* in which things are said is just as important as *what* is said. This has all too often been overlooked. Just as the construction of a building comes from carefully following the blueprint for its design, so our spiritual lives have a blueprint as well. Better than any other letters, Romans and Ephesians give us that blueprint.

Ephesians very clearly has three major sections. Each section has a radically different emphasis and calling. And they build one upon the other. The first major section is Eph.1:1-3:21 and the emphasis is upon "*the heavenlies*" (Eph. 1:3,20; 2:6; 3:10.) **The great calling of these first three chapters is for all believers to be caught up in passionate, knowledgeable, first-hand encountering and worshipping of the triune God.** Not surprisingly, our first calling is supremely God-ward; for it is truly the foundation and heartbeat of all vital spirituality.

The second major section is Eph. 4:1-6:9, and it is a radical shift from the first section. The great emphasis of this section is found in its key word: "*walk,*" (Eph. 4:1, 17; 5:2, 8, 15.) **The great calling of this section is for all believers to live surprising lives while stationed upon this earth.** To live in such a way that others are blindsided by unexpected glimpses of the supernatural in the most practical and ordinary facets of daily living. From marriage, to parenting, to church life, to the working world, all are to be utilized for Kingdom purposes. The shift is now from the vertical to the horizontal, from the heavenlies to the earthlies, if you will. St. Francis of Assisi's famous statement perfectly encapsulates this second major section of Ephesians: "*Preach the gospel at all times. If necessary, use words.*"

It would be easy to think that the letter ends there. After all, what more could God want than believers who are glutting themselves in all the fullness of the Godhead, and then supernaturally reflecting that fullness while they faithfully pursue their opportunities and responsibilities on earth with an eye single to God's glory? They are loving their God well and loving their neighbors well, both the saved and the unsaved. What else could there possibly be?

This is what I find so intriguing and important. There is an entire third sphere besides heaven and earth which we would probably completely walk past if Paul didn't rein us back in. That sphere? Hell itself. And our calling toward that sphere is found in Eph. 6:10-24, the third great section of Ephesians. *"Finally, my brethren, be strong in the Lord and in the power of His might. Put on the whole armor of God, that you may be able to stand against the wiles of the devil. For we do not wrestle against flesh and blood, but against principalities, against powers, against the rulers of the darkness of this age, against spiritual hosts of wickedness in the heavenly places," (*Eph. 6:10-12.)

The great calling of this section is for all believers to do hand-to-hand combat against the spiritual forces of Satan's

domain. In fact the Greek word used in this passage for "*wrestle*" is a word that was used especially in reference to hand-to-hand combat. This is a warfare that absolutely requires "*the whole armor of God,*" as described in the rest of Eph. 6:13-18. Mere mortals, even though redeemed by the blood of the true King, dare not go into warfare such as this without His weaponry.

This third major section of Ephesians is the shortest—Eph. 6:10-24. But that doesn't mean it isn't vitally important. Nor that it is a kind of optional, extra-credit addendum to the two sections which have preceded it. No, a thousand times no! Charles Spurgeon put it well, "*To be a Christian is to be a warrior. The good soldier of Jesus Christ must not expect to find ease in this world: it is a battle-field. Neither must he reckon upon the friendship of the world; for that would be enmity against God. His occupation is war. As he puts on piece by piece of the panoply provided for him, he may wisely say to himself, 'This warns me of danger; this prepares me for warfare; this prophesies opposition.*'"

It is normative for every believer to be a gate crasher, daily storming the gates of hell. Storming them by bold, persistent prayer for others. Storming them by winsome, Christ-scented responses to mistreatment. Storming them by humble, respectful verbalizing of the gospel to those asking "*...a reason for the hope that is in you...*" (I Pet. 3:15) Storming them by providing hope and tangible support for unwed mothers. Storming them by helping free the victims of sex-slave trafficking. Storming them by visiting geriatric centers and loving the world's forgotten. Storming them by beginning a bible study at your workplace or in your neighborhood. Storming them by giving generously to those parts of the world where the gospel is most absent. Storming them by mentoring younger believers in the faith. Storming them by loving the Lord with all that we are and our neighbor as ourselves. Storming them by becoming a game changer in others' lives. This is what I mean by "Dangerous Christianity."

Nobody, but nobody, graduates from Ephesians without becoming dangerous. Without going to war. Without becoming a threat to the kingdom of darkness. Without becoming both a *game changer* and a *gate crasher.* This is normative Christianity. For the first three centuries of the church, this was the routine job description belonging to all Christ-followers. Michael Green, in his outstanding work "Evangelism in the Early Church," writes of these early believers, *"Christianity for them was no hour's slot on a Sunday. It affected everything they did and everyone they met. Their church life was warm and nourishing, for the most part, and equipped people to move out with the good news. The ordinary Christians, the missionaries, the academics, the women, all seem to have shared in this same passionate commitment to the cause."* And there is absolutely no good reason why it shouldn't be the same today. Or why it couldn't be. Anything less is a dumbing down of our temporary, earthly job assignment. How dangerous are you, my friend? How dangerous am I? The rest of this book is devoted to the fulfillment of Jim Elliot's cry, *"Oh that God would make us dangerous!"*

Chapter 2

Revisiting the Battlefield

Some wish to live within the sound of Church or Chapel bell; I want to run a Rescue Shop within a yard of hell.
—C. T. Studd

Nobody saw it coming. Nestled beside the Aegean Sea, Thessalonica was a great city to live in during the first century. Prosperous, self-governing, and elite among the cities of Macedonia, it had everything going for it. Religiously diverse, Thessalonica was composed of a mixture of pagan religions with enough Jews to warrant a synagogue. The city was flourishing, families were thriving, and life was good for the vast majority of its citizens. There was, however, one thing missing. There were no—I repeat—no followers of Jesus. The gates of Hades appeared to be prevailing. But all that would change dramatically in a very short time.

Around the year 51 AD, three men strolled into the city. Three men whom God would use to rock the entire metropolis and cause an uproar among its citizens. Three men who would be part of a perceived cult so infectious that it would be said of them, "*…these who have turned the world upside down have come here too,*" (Acts 17:6.) Three men who would leave in their wake one of the most dynamic churches of the New Testament. Three dangerous disciples, three gate crashers, three game changers. Yet three men who were every bit as flawed, fallen, and human as you and me. Let me introduce you to Paul, Silas, and Timothy. Let me also introduce you to their battlefield, the city of Thessalonica. Most of all, let me introduce you to their stratagems for vital, life-transforming, Christ-spotlighting ministry.

I pick what happened at Thessalonica for two important reasons. First, it was either Paul's first or second letter, depending on how one dates Galatians. This really doesn't matter. In either case, it is the first letter that details Paul's specific battle plan for establishing the most significant beachhead for the gospel ever devised by God—the local church. I Thess. 1:1-2:12 gives us the very heartbeat of Paul's approach to ministry—not only in Thessalonica, but wherever he went. Therefore, I believe there is much more to this section than simply Paul's rehashing what happened with the Thessalonians. **While it serves to not only recount the past, it becomes also a template for the future.** He expected that the Thessalonians would use these same stratagems in their own ongoing ministry toward others. Which they did. Frankly, I believe this is one of the greatly overlooked gems of scripture. It lets us in on the original game plan. No ministry can afford to miss being steeped in the principles and truths these verses hold out. Sadly, however, too many are by-passing the original marching orders for newer, quicker, glitzier methods which have everything to offer except the supernatural touch of God.

Secondly, this blueprint is never altered! For about the next thirty years Paul roamed the world of his day, repeating in city after city the same basic battle plan he used in Thessalonica. It never changes except in very minor details. And it helps make Paul very possibly the most dangerous Christian who has ever lived (other than our Lord, of course.) For the next three hundred years the church would use this same battle plan, resulting in the greatest gospel penetration this world has ever known. Around the beginning of the fourth century, with the installation of Constantine as emperor, the church began veering away from this original blueprint. Before too long, it had veered significantly. Consequently, its vitality and influence began to diminish. Therefore, we do well to seek to understand and implement this original stratagem as well as possible. I believe you will find in the history of the church that this stratagem, whenever followed, has almost always borne significant fruit to the glory of God.

In light of this, there is one other group besides the early Christians that I will also focus on throughout this book—the Moravians. Founded in 1722 by Count Nicolaus von Zinzendorf and a handful of fellow believers, this band of Kingdom radicals grew dynamically and significantly influenced many, many unreached parts of the world with the gospel for about the next 150 years. Perhaps no other movement post 300 AD has followed Paul's stratagem as closely as these amazing saints. Colin Grant, chairman of the Evangelical Alliance writes concerning the Moravians, "*The Unitas Fratum (United Brethren), as they had been called, have left a record without parallel in the post-New Testament era of world evangelization, and we do well to look again at the main characteristics of this movement and learn the lessons God has for us.*"

In our day of mega churches, mega leaders, and mega programs, I Thessalonians beckons us to have the courage to radically rethink how we are doing church. Or perhaps better, how we are not doing church. The reason the para-church ministries (Cru, Navigators, YWAM, Young Life, etc.) have often been monumentally more impactful for the gospel than many established churches is very simple. **They are following the original blueprint far more closely than these established churches.** And as a result they are also experiencing God's hand of blessing far more significantly. I would say the same thing about the church in China with its explosive growth from 1949 until today. They are simply following the original game plan. In fact, they are often following it more closely than many of the western missionaries did; who served there prior to 1949.

More recently, the explosive growth of evangelicals in New York City has demonstrated the stunning power of following the original blueprint. In 1989, less than 1% of all New Yorkers were attending gospel-centered churches. Under the strong influence of Tim Keller and others, in 2016 that number has skyrocketed to over 5% of all New Yorkers. These church leaders presently are working toward and praying for the audacious goal of 15% by the year 2026!

Without a doubt, there are places all over the world where local churches are being used by God in breathtaking ways. In fact, there are probably far more of them than any of us are aware of. However, as one writer put it, the church too often is storming the gates of hell with water pistols! Annie Dillard puts it marvelously, *"On the whole, I do not find Christians, outside of the catacombs, sufficiently sensible of conditions. Does anyone have the foggiest idea what sort of power we so blithely invoke? Or, as I suspect, does no one believe a word of it? The churches are children playing on the floor with their chemistry sets, mixing up a batch of TNT to kill a Sunday morning. It is madness to wear ladies' straw hats and velvet hats to church; we should all be wearing crash helmets. Ushers should issue life preservers and signal flares; they should lash us to our pews. For the sleeping god may wake someday and take offense, or the waking god may draw us out to where we can never return."*

Far too many churches and Christian organizations are missing out on the divinely intended impact bestowed upon them by resurrection power. Unwittingly and unintentionally, we find ourselves playing almost completely in our own sandbox and have become so irrelevant to our present world that we don't even recognize how irrelevant we have become. As one writer put it, "*We have become church busy, but influence barren.*" The great news is that it doesn't need to remain this way! These passages in I Thessalonians speak with remarkable directness and hope to any and all believers whose hearts are stirred to become gate crashers and game changers. Those who have gone before us have proven that the strategy works, and they have now taken their seats with the "*so great a cloud of witnesses*" (Heb. 12:1), cheering us on to follow in their go-for-broke footsteps. But before we turn to I Thessalonians, we do well to first turn to Acts 17 in order to revisit the battlefield of Thessalonica and see what we can learn from victories of long ago.

Stratagem 1 Take the initiative.

"*Now when they had passed through Amphipolis and Apollonia, they came to Thessalonica...*" (Acts 17:1)

They "*passed through*" two cities—Amphipolis and Apollonia. They stopped however when "*they came to Thessalonica.*" Why? One reason may stem from the fact that neither Amphipolis nor Apollonia had synagogues. In any case, we find throughout Paul's life that he was very careful where he chose to plant churches. He always picked cities that had significant contact with the rest of the world and were nestled along the heavy trade routes of the day. We find an important principle here that colored the whole of Paul's life. **Dangerous Christians learn to by-pass the good for the best**. In our service for God, most decisions are not between good and bad. The vast majority are between good and best. Not every open door is the best to be walked through, not every opportunity is worthy of seizing. Paul's prayer for the Philippians illustrates this well, "*that you may approve the things that are excellent,*" (Phil. 1:10.) The good is often the worst enemy of the best, and dangerous Christians keep this in mind as they navigate where and how to spend their time and effort.

But most important is the issue of initiative. Note it doesn't say when they were invited to Thessalonica. They simply *came.* **Dangerous Christians do not wait to be invited to do ministry.** They just go. The gates of Hades are remarkably reluctant to issue invitations for invasion. Paul was never invited to any of the places he went! He just took the initiative and went...utterly uninvited. And so it is to this day.

Over a period of 150 years, the Moravians sent 2,158 of its own members to lands all over the world to make known the gospel...without one single invitation. They just went. The first two, John Leonard Dober and David Nitschman, sailed to the West Indies in order to get the gospel to the slaves there. They went so uninvited that that they fully expected to sell themselves into slavery so that they could work side by side with the other slaves as they shared Christ with them!

More recently, when Jim Rayburn was burdened for the plight of high school kids, he went to the schools...uninvited. Thus Young Life was born. When Bill Bright felt the need to reach out to university students, he went to the universities... uninvited. Enter Campus Crusade for Christ. When William Carey became burdened by the great need for the gospel in India, he went...uninvited. And there he labored for over seven years amidst much opposition before he saw his first convert. When my dear friend Walt Baker, a seminary professor, wanted to have gospel impact in the school's surrounding neighborhood, he consistently went to the local Starbucks...uninvited. And over time he has had tremendous influence on many of those frequenting that establishment. The places that need the gospel the most are highly unlikely to issue invitations to come. Your workplace will probably never invite you to begin a lunch bible study within its confines. But that is just the arena where the gospel is so badly needed. The president of your homeowners association is highly unlikely to ever invite you to launch an evangelistic study in your neighborhood. But that is just the place where the gospel needs to be. Trust me as a pastor; we pretty much have all the bible studies we need safely secluded within the four walls of church buildings. Not that there is anything wrong with this. But what we most need are battlefield bible studies, led by dangerous Christians—men and women willing to leave their comfort zones and venture into the risky waters of where the fish actually live. And where the gospel is most needed. Scottish pastor George MacLeod put it so well:

"I simply argue that the cross be raised again at the center of the marketplace as well as on the steeple of the church. I am recovering the claim that Jesus was not crucified in a cathedral between two candles, but on a cross between two thieves; on the town garbage heap; at a crossroad so cosmopolitan that they had to write His title in Hebrew and in Latin and in Greek; at the kind of place where cynics talk smut, and thieves curse, and soldiers gamble. Because that is where He died. And that is what He died about. That is where church-men ought to be and what church- men ought to be about."

I love his last line, *"That is where church-men ought to be and what church- men ought to be about."* It certainly was what Paul was about.

Stratagem 2 Maximize our natural sphere of influence.

"*...where there was a synagogue of the Jews. Then Paul, as his custom was, went in to them...*" (Acts 17:1,2)

Somewhere write down "natural sphere of influence." **Dangerous Christians maximize their natural sphere of influence.** Paul was the apostle specifically called to go to the Gentiles (Gal. 2:8; Rom. 15:16.) No doubt about it. But everywhere new that Paul went, he went first of all to the synagogue and his fellow Jews (Acts 13:5,14; Acts 14:1; Acts 17:1,17; Acts 18:4; Acts 19:8.) No doubt about it. "*...as his custom was...*" Why?

One important reason was that he understood that God's chosen people (the Jews) had first dibs on the gospel, so to speak. This is why he writes concerning the gospel, "*...for it is the power of God to salvation for everyone who believes, for the Jew first and also for the Greek,*" (Rom. 1:16 also Acts 28:25-28.) Therefore, he was responsible to go first to "*...the lost sheep of the house of Israel,*" as our Lord commanded (Mtt. 10:6.) Another reason was probably that it was in the synagogue he had the best chance of encountering the most spiritually interested of the city. It was the main place where the practicing Jews and Gentile "God fearers" would congregate.

But there was more to it than just these two reasons. Far more. Paul understood that his background was not accidental but sovereign. That God was the One Who had determined his heritage, his parents, his ethnicity, and his DNA. He also recognized that his gifts, upbringing, accomplishments, position, etc., were all collective parts of God's sovereign weaving of his life, and that these qualities afforded him a unique and divinely-crafted sphere of influence. And that this sphere of influence was his most immediate mission field—his Jerusalem, if you will. As J. Oswald Sanders put it, "*God never wastes our background.*" In other words, the uniqueness of our background provides us with a unique bridge into the unbelieving world. A bridge which no one else can exactly walk over. Dangerous Christians fully maximize that bridge.

There is a fascinating passage in Mk. 5 which speaks very directly to this issue. In Mk. 5:1-20 we have the description of Christ healing and transforming the Gerasene demoniac. As

Jesus and the disciples are getting ready to leave, we read, *"And when He got into the boat, he who had been demon-possessed begged Him that he might be with Him,"* (Mk. 5:18.) Who could blame this man for wanting to go with Jesus? After all, this was the One who had healed him, loved him, and utterly transformed him. But notice our Lord's response. *"However, Jesus did not permit him, but said to him, 'Go home to your friends, and tell them what great things the Lord has done for you, and how He has had compassion on you,'"* (Mk. 5:19.)

The phrase that is translated "*your friends*" literally means "those who are yours." In other words, "those who belong to you." How fascinating! And how important as well! There is clearly a stewardship issue at stake here. "Those who are yours" means those whom you and I have unique responsibility towards, those who fall within our immediate sphere of influence, those whom God has sovereignly entrusted to be next to us. Many translations have "your own people." So what's the point?

Time, treasure, and talent. Ever hear a message on these three? You can't attend church very long without hearing a message on this triad. These are the big three. They all fall under the heading of "stewardship" and any message on stewardship worth its salt includes them. And rightly so, for they clearly are three vital areas which God has entrusted to us to faithfully steward. I don't for a minute want to take anything away from the legitimacy and importance of these.

But this passage in Mark is clearly indicating another area of stewardship that seems to be very rarely talked about. Since the Christian world seems to be addicted to alliteration, I'll give another "t:" territory. Time, treasure, talent, and territory. There are certain people on this planet who are as much a part of our stewardship as the way we use our time, our money, and our talents. They are the people whom God has seen fit to bring into our lives for His transforming purposes. We are uniquely connected to these people in ways that other believers are not. They are first and foremost our family, then our friends, our co-workers, our neighbors, our tennis partners, our fishing buddies, our fellow club members, etc. One of the main reasons Paul went first to the Jews in a new city was because he was uniquely connected to them. He had been entrusted with a rich Jewish heritage, wonderful Jewish training, and great Jewish accomplishments (Phil. 3:4-6.) All of these enabled him to be uniquely connected to a group of people which others could not. And this sovereignly-crafted background also made him uniquely responsible to see that this group got "gospeled" by his life and speech. And like Paul, every one of us is uniquely connected to unbelievers who need to be blindsided by the same Jesus who blindsided us. And we cannot blindside them very well while keeping our distance.

I was playing tennis a few years ago with a friend when we began discussing church and Christianity during one of our breaks. I'll never forget what he said. "My biggest problem with this 'born again' thing is that every friend I've ever had who got 'saved', I barely ever saw again. It wasn't that they were mad at me or had moved somewhere different or anything like that. It was just that they didn't have time for me anymore. They were so tied up with their church activities that they were never free to meet me for Happy Hour, go out to a movie, or even play tennis together." As I listened to his words I winced. Not only because of his experience, but because of the all too many years that I had been guilty that very same thing.

My first job out of college was as a teaching tennis pro at the Midland Country Club in Texas. It was a fantastic place to work, filled with wonderful people, many of whom were not believers. Before long I was steeped in ministry. I taught a Sunday school class at our church, discipled some students, became very involved with Young Life, etc. But in the two years I was there I never once took a fellow pro out to dinner. Never once met a club member for a drink (though I was often invited.) Never once took the initiative to go see a movie with someone from the club. But all the while I was spending all kinds of time in ministry toward others in the city. I had leapfrogged my primary mission field and focused on a secondary one which I was far less naturally connected with.

When I went into the pastorate I spent way too many years completely covered over with other believers, rarely spending any significant time with unsaved in my natural sphere of influence. Now I make sure that I spend a significant amount of time with unbelievers whom I am most naturally connected with. My only regret is that I didn't see this sooner.

One of the significant reasons for the amazing impact the early Christians had on their world was that they took this natural sphere of influence so seriously and naturally. Michael Green writes, "*This* (evangelism*) must often have been not formal preaching, but informal chattering to friends and chance acquaintances, in homes and wine shops, on walks, and around market stalls. They* *went everywhere gossiping the gospel; they did it naturally, enthusiastically, and with the conviction of those who are not paid to say that sort of thing. Consequently, they were taken seriously…"* I love his phrase, *"They went everywhere gossiping the gospel."* And they gossiped it first and foremost to those in their natural sphere of influence.

Who are "those who are yours?" They are those individuals whom we are most naturally connected to, those people to whom we are their nearest significant Christian contact. When Matthew began following Jesus, the first thing he did was expose his natural sphere of influence to his Savior. *"After these things He went out and saw a tax collector named Levi, sitting at the tax office. And He said to him, 'Follow Me.' So he left all, rose up, and followed Him. Then Levi gave Him a great feast in his own house. And there were a great number of tax collectors and others who sat down with them,"* (Lk.5:27-29.) When Andrew began following Christ, he did the same and exposed his brother to the Messiah. "*He **first** found his own brother Simon, and said to him, "We have found the Messiah," (which is translated, the Christ.) And he brought him to Jesus," (Jn. 1:41, 42.)*

These connections may be through family, work, neighborhood, sports, a shared hobby, Junior League, school board, or a host of other divinely-crafted opportunities. These connections often vary wildly from one believer to another. But one thing is for sure—connections are not accidental! The One Who "*works all things according to the counsel of His will,*" (Eph. 1:11) has sovereignly fitted each of us for the exact spot He wants us to occupy on the battlefront. He has placed in our foxhole those specific individuals whom He wants to touch and transform through our yielded bodies. This begins with the most difficult mission field of all—our family.

Christiana Tsai, a Chinese national, sought to introduce her family to the Savior Who had so changed her life. At first they were very hardened and resistant. But she simply kept loving them and walking with her Lord. One day, one of her brothers who had rejected the gospel, assembled the members of the family without them knowing the purpose behind it. He then told them, *"I have been to see Christiana many times and wondered how she could endure all this suffering. Now I can see that she has been given some sustaining power and can only explain it as coming from God. So, I have decided there must be a God after all. I have read the Bible and realize that I am a sinner. So here and now I want to tell you that I have accepted Christ as my Savior, asked Him to forgive my sins, and promised to follow Him."*

Christiana commented that, *"The brother who tore up my Bible and persecuted me in the early days at last confessed my Lord. In all, fifty-five of my relatives have become God's children and expressed their faith in Jesus. I have never been to college, or theological seminary, and I am not a Bible teacher; I have only been God's hunting dog."* I love that! And the hunt began with her most immediate sphere of influence, her family.

God has carefully insured that we each have a divinely-orchestrated background that uniquely equips us to reach others with a similar background. Like Paul, we all have a synagogue that has first dibs on us. And marching orders to maximize it. This is where gate crashing and game changing begins.

Way, way too many Christians today are waiting for ministry to be handed to them. They are waiting to be asked to teach a Sunday School, lead a home church, become a deacon or elder, etc. And when this doesn't happen, they bemoan the fact that there's no place for them to serve. Paul and the early Christians would have been completely mystified by this. They all understood that a vital ministry had already been handed to them—their natural sphere of influence. And that God had already clearly given the green light to proceed forward…with abandon!

Stratagem 3 Maximize the Word of God, Spotlight the Son of God, Humbly communicate the Message of God.

"…and for three Sabbaths reasoned with them from the Scriptures, explaining and demonstrating that the Christ had to suffer and rise again from the dead, and saying, "This Jesus whom I preach to you is the Christ," (Acts 17:2, 3)

We find here three stunningly powerful weapons utilized by Paul for blasting through the gate of Hades entitled "Thessalonica." Simply put, he laser-focused upon the Son of God by setting forth the word of God. And he did it with the humility of a wildly-graced sinner inviting fellow sinners to the same astonishing banquet table where he was feasting. **Dangerous Christians make sure their message is Christ-focused, scripture-saturated, and humbly-communicated.**

First we see that Paul was extraordinarily careful with the focus of his message. He didn't spend his verbal ammunition on what was wrong with the Thessalonians, the Jews, or their culture. His white-hot focus was on what was right with Christ. "*…Christ had to suffer and rise again from the dead…This Jesus…*

is the Christ." Paul understood well that nothing arrests the mind, melts the heart, and transforms the life like the relentless spotlighting of a Person. The Person. The only Person Who ever loved men enough to die for their sins and was powerful enough to rise from the dead. If the Thessalonians were going to reject the gospel, he wanted to be sure that they knew that they were not simply turning down a new and innovative teaching. He wanted them to know they were turning down a Person. A Person bringing them the unconditional offer of being loved every day of their lives with a love they could find nowhere else. And the opportunity to have the most breath-taking Person in the universe actually invade the deep citadel of their hearts and take up glad residence within.

What a badly needed reminder for the church today! So much of our preaching and teaching is what C. John Miller aptly calls in his outstanding book *Outgrowing the Ingrown Church*, "joyless moralism." All too often the sermon is essentially a lecture on keeping the rules of the club, the blessings of keeping those rules, and the consequences for not doing so. David Brainerd, one of the very first missionaries to the American Indians discovered the incredible power of focusing preeminently upon the Person rather than the rules. *"I never got away from Jesus, and Him crucified, and I found that when my people were gripped by this great evangelical doctrine of Christ and Him crucified, I had no need to give them instructions about morality. I found that one followed as the sure and inevitable fruit of the other...I find my Indians begin to put on the garments of holiness and their common life begins to be sanctified even in small matters when they are possessed by the doctrine of Christ and Him crucified."*

No doubt there were occasions where he gave them "*instructions about morality.*" But these instructions were always the natural result of his primary invitation to come enjoy a Person. Reinhold Niebuhr put it so well, *"You may be able to compel people to maintain certain minimum standards by stressing duty, but the highest moral and spiritual achievements depend not upon a push but a pull. People must be charmed into righteousness."* Nothing charms people into righteousness more than having their breath taken away by the wonder and awe of the true and living God. **Dangerous Christians are more concerned with helping people fall in love with Jesus than making sure they are following the rules.** This is why Paul was such a continual thorn in the side of the legalists.

The Moravians were complete zealots concerning focusing on Christ in their presentations. Dr. Kenneth Mulholland writes, *"Zinzendorf counseled outgoing missionaries, 'You must go straight to the point and tell them about the life and death of Christ.' Earlier missionaries had often given elaborate proofs for the existence of God as though they were giving theology lectures. Zinzendorf urged the missionaries simply to tell the story of Jesus. There are numerous accounts of how that story awakened slumbering hearts and brought them to the Savior."*

One such incident is recorded by Dr. David Ryoo, "*There was a turning point which caused them to emphasize the story of Jesus. In spite of several years of hard work, missionaries in Greenland did not convert any natives. However, the time came when the message of the missionaries was received. They abandoned preaching abstract theological doctrine and simply preached Jesus Christ, and their first successes followed immediately. When Kajarnak, a native of Greenland, heard the story of Jesus, he came forward with his eager question, 'What is that? Tell me that again.' The native broke the silence and indifference by showing his interest in the story of Jesus."* There is extraordinary, extraordinary power in staying centered on the person of Christ. This is true not only for justification, but for sanctification as well.

Second, we find that Paul was unswerving regarding the content of his message, *"...reasoned with them from the Scriptures."* Dangerous Christians are fanatical about getting the naked, unedited, undiluted word of God into people's consciousness. We will deal with this in much greater detail in upcoming chapters. Suffice it to say for right now, Paul understood that it is only the word of God which is *"living and powerful, and sharper than any two-edged sword, piercing even to the division of soul and spirit,"* (Heb. 4:12.) It is only the word of God that is *"a fire and a hammer that breaks the rock into pieces,"* (Jer. 23:29.) It is only the word of God that contains the promise, *"So shall My word be that goes forth from My mouth; it shall not return to Me void, but it shall accomplish what I please, and it shall prosper in the thing for which I sent it,"* (Is. 55:11.) This is why Paul's final words to his disciple Timothy contained the charge, *"Preach the word,"* (II Tim. 4:2.) Not preach about the word, not preach around the word, but preach the word. When Martin Luther described his reason for success in ministry he noted,

"For the Word created heaven and earth and all things [Ps. 33:6]; the Word must do this thing, and not we poor sinners.

In short, I will preach it, teach it, write it, but I will constrain no man by force, for faith must come freely without compulsion. Take myself as an example...I simply taught, preached, and wrote God's Word; otherwise I did nothing. And while I slept [cf. Mark 4:26–29], or drank Wittenberg beer with my friends Philipp and Amsdorf, the Word so greatly weakened the papacy that no prince or emperor ever inflicted such losses upon it. I did nothing; the Word did everything. Had I desired to foment trouble, I could have brought great bloodshed upon Germany; indeed, I could have started such a game that even the emperor would not have been safe. But what would it have been? Mere fool's play. I did nothing; I let the Word do its work…But when we spread the Word alone and let it alone do the work that distresses him (the devil.) For it is almighty, and takes captive the hearts, and when the hearts are captured the work will fall of itself."

The word of God in open circulation is one of the most dangerous threats there is to the gates of Hades. No wonder Satan does everything possible to keep it under wraps.

Third, note the manner in which Paul communicated to the Thessalonians. It was that oh-so-powerful combination of truth expressed in humility and grace. Truth is most powerfully communicated through broken vessels. Notice the verbs: *"reasoned with them…explaining and demonstrating…"* **Dangerous Christians refuse to talk *down* to their listeners, but rather talk *with* them in a spirit of profound humility.** The word used for "*reasoned*" was used to describe the Socratic question and answer approach to communicating truth. The phrase "*explaining and demonstrating*" literally means "opening and placing before." We find that Paul did not come to the Thessalonians to set them straight. He came to invite them to explore the word of God with him and see if perhaps their Messiah was not, in fact, Jesus of Nazareth. In no way did he compromise the truth through his humility, but neither did he obscure the truth through religious arrogance. He spotlighted the scriptures and the Savior, while relishing his role to simply remain in the shadows. His message was virtually identical to that of the Samaritan woman as she went back to the people of her village, *"Come, see a Man who told me all things that I ever did. Could this be the Christ?"* (Jn.4:29.) I love, but love the way she puts this. She doesn't scold them or preach to them. She *invites* them!

Dangerous Christians don't scold, they invite. They invite people to a Person, not a set of rules. Simply put, they invite them to trade up. Few men have exemplified this spirit of humility and respect in communicating divine truth better than C.S. Lewis. You can read all his works and you will never once feel talked down to. It is one of the things that make his writings so powerful. Once asked some advice, he wrote back and kindly gave it. But then he added, *"Think of me as a fellow-patient in the same hospital who, having been admitted a little earlier, could give some advice."*

This is the exact attitude we all should have in ministering to others! Alexander Maclaren put it so well, *"The only way to help people is to get to their level... If you want to bless men, you must identify yourself with them. It is no use standing on an eminence above them, and patronizingly talking down to them. You cannot scold, or hector, or lecture men into the possession and acceptance of religious truth if you take a position of superiority. As our Master has taught us, if we want to make blind beggars see we must take the blind beggars by the hand."* Dangerous Christians truly, truly believe that they are fellow patients with everyone else in the hospital of life. Our spiritual ailments and injuries may vary, but we are no less in need of the Doctor's care than anyone else we come in contact with. Our cancer may be better hidden and more respectable than that of others, but it is no less cancer and we are no less patients. Dangerous Christians are careful to keep their profound awareness of this intact. To the end of days they passionately believe they are simply one beggar telling other beggars where they found bread.

Just as an aside, I would also say this in regards to the danger of talking down to people as we are seeking to minister to them: **this present generation will not be talked down to.** Let me say it another way—nothing turns our new generation off more quickly than being preached down to. This is a HUGE issue for being a spiritual game changer in this day and time. The overbearing, scolding style of preaching which was tolerated and even expected in previous generations will not see the light of day with our present generation. Past generations didn't like being talked down to, but we tolerated it for the most part. Today's generation will not tolerate it. If they sense us talking down to them from our lofty perch of supposed spiritual superiority, they will completely tune us out. And frankly, I don't blame them. But if we will come alongside as fellow strugglers, respecting their thoughts and opinions, sharing (not preaching down) what God has taught us, for the most part they will give us their ear. And perhaps they will give Jesus their hearts as well.

What was the result of these stratagems? Basically two things: revival and revolt. The same sun that melts the wax also hardens the clay. That is exactly what happened in Thessalonica and almost every place that Paul went for that matter.

The heat of the gospel melted the softened hearts of many, and they responded in faith. "*And some of them were persuaded; and a great multitude of the devout Greeks, and not a few of the leading women, joined Paul and Silas,*" (Acts 17:4.) Never, ever underestimate the astonishing power of the word of God and the gospel message. Notice who among this group responded: *not a few of the leading ladies.* This is amazing! These leading ladies of society had absolutely nothing to gain by joining this new cult. Their social standing would soon plummet, their relationships with their husbands would be severely strained to say the least, and they might even be imprisoned. But when one's heart is melted by the love of Christ and pierced through by the word of God, even the gates of hades can no longer keep that person in check.

Others, however, hardened themselves to the same message and became antagonistic. *"But the Jews who were not persuaded, becoming envious, took some of the evil men from the marketplace, and gathering a mob, set all the city in an uproar and attacked the house of Jason, and sought to bring them out to the people. But when they did not find them, they dragged Jason and some brethren to the rulers of the city, crying out, 'These who have turned the world upside down have come here too. Jason has harbored them, and these are all acting contrary to the decrees of Caesar, saying there is another king—Jesus.' And they troubled the crowd and the rulers of the city when they heard these things. So when they had taken security from Jason and the rest, they let them go,"* (Acts 17:5-9.)

When the word of God is well-dispensed, when the Son of God is well-spotlighted, and when the humble servant of God is well-utilized, we find that men and women are either drawn to the aroma of the gospel or repelled by what they consider to be a stench. This is exactly what Paul was referring to when he wrote, *"Now thanks be to God who always leads us in triumph in Christ, and through us diffuses the fragrance of His knowledge in every place. For we are to God the fragrance of Christ among those who are being saved and among those who are perishing. To the one we are the aroma of death leading to death, and to the other the aroma of life leading to life,"* (II Cor. 2:14-16.)

Dangerous Christians are game changers. They are gate crashers. But above all else, they are first and foremost Christ-lovers. White hot, recklessly abandoned, utterly enthralled Christ-lovers. And that, more than any other reason, is the reason their lives are so precarious to the enemy.

Chapter 3

The Front Line of Attack

The one concern of the Devil is to keep the saints from praying. He fears nothing from prayer-less studies, prayer-less work, prayer-less religion. He laughs at our toil, mocks at our wisdom, but trembles when we pray.
—Samuel Chadwick

SOMEONE HAS WELL NOTED, "*A man's words are the ambassadors of his soul.*" What we are on the inside is inevitably represented by the words we let loose on the outside. No doubt this is true. And in the opening two verses of Paul's words to the Thessalonians, we find two statements that give us significant insight into the heart and character of this extraordinarily dangerous saint. He was a man who went to war in lock step with other Kingdom radicals and a soldier who desperately depended upon prayer as his front line of attack. And was not afraid to say so.

A man of community

"Paul, Silvanus, and Timothy, to the church of the Thessalonians in God the Father and the Lord Jesus Christ: Grace to you and peace from God our Father and the Lord Jesus Christ. (I Thess. 1:1)

The first thing to note is simply this—**dangerous Christians never work alone.** If anyone could have made a difference for Christ solo, surely it was Paul. Extraordinarily gifted, superbly trained, laser-focused, and having been taught personally by

Christ, it would have been desperately easy for Paul to have winged it on his own. But just as it takes two wings to fly, it takes two or more saints to accomplish God's work, God's way. This is why we read, "*Paul, Silvanus, and Timothy.*" Every genuine work of God is always a group project even when great leaders are part of the group. Our Lord was careful to send out His disciples in pairs, (Mk. 6:7.) The Moravian missionaries always went out in at least pairs.

There are many reasons for this, but I am going to confine myself to only four of them. First, **we all need helping hands to stay the course**. Solomon put it best: *"Two are better than one, because they have a good reward for their labor. For if they fall, one will lift up his companion. But woe to him who is alone when he falls, for he has no one to help him up. Again, if two lie down together, they will keep warm; but how can one be warm alone? Though one may be overpowered by another, two can withstand him. And a threefold cord is not quickly broken,"* (Ecc. 4:9-12.)

Notice the different benefits from this passage of not trying to fly solo. Increased productivity, help getting back on one's feet, mutual warmth, and victory over opposition. In a word, *we need each other.* And never do we need each other more than when going to war! This is exactly the scenario we find in this verse. These are not three vacationers enjoying the sights and sounds of Thessalonica. Nor three savvy businessmen looking to profit in the marketplaces of the city. Nor even three humanitarians seeking to meet the physical needs of the underserved of the city.

These are three men going to war! Gate crashers who are walking straight into the jaws of hell, bringing divinely supplied ammunition for the attack, and expecting that they will be covering each other's backs before the battle is over. They indeed became a threefold cord which proved too sturdy to break.

Second, **our own spiritual growth is immeasurably enhanced by close connection with other believers.** One of my favorite passages concerning this is found in David's relationship with Jonathan. *"Then Jonathan, Saul's son, arose and went to David in the woods and strengthened his hand in God,"* (I Sam. 23:16.) Notice it doesn't say that he strengthened David's hand. It says he strengthened David's hand *in God.* There is a huge difference between the two. While we all need encouragement and strengthening, we need something else even more. We need believers who are able to enter our world, place our hand in God's hand, and then step back out. These dear saints, few as they usually are in most believers' lives, truly give us the gift that keeps on giving. The gift of refusing to merely hold our hand until we feel a bit better; but holding our hand long enough to place it in the strong, sovereign grip of the only One in our lives who truly will never leave us nor forsake us.

We need other believers not only for strengthening but also for learning. Dangerous Christians are anything but isolated, self-taught saints. They have dropped their intellectual and spiritual arrogance in favor of a winsome brokenness that is eager to learn through any of God's instruments. C.S. Lewis articulated this so well:

"My own experience is that when I first became a Christian, about fourteen years ago, I thought that I could do it on my own, by retiring to my rooms and reading theology, and I wouldn't go to

the churches and Gospel Halls;...I disliked very much their hymns, which I considered to be fifth-rate poems set to sixth-rate music. But as I went on I saw the great merit of it. I came up against different people of quite different outlooks and different education, and then gradually my conceit just began peeling off. I realized that the hymns (which were just sixth-rate music) were, nevertheless, being sung with devotion and benefit by an old saint in elastic-side boots in the opposite pew, and then you realize that you aren't fit to clean those boots. It gets you out of your solitary conceit."

What a great last sentence! "*It gets you out of your solitary conceit.*" Is this not in large measure what spiritual growth is all about? Moving out of our own noxious, smug, independent arrogance into the joyous, humble, radical other-centeredness which so characterized our Lord. Among the primary tools God employs are the saints He places around us, who, like paint-brushes, spread His stunning colors upon our lives.

Third, **the true effectiveness of any ministry is dependent upon each member playing to their own strength.** What I mean by this is that a huge part of doing God's work God's way is exploiting our primary spiritual gift to its fullest. Spiritual gifts are a big issue in the New Testament. A really big issue. While, like in Corinth, they can be abused in various ways, by far the greatest abuse in the church today is neglect. Neglect in knowing one's spiritual gift. Neglect in using one's spiritual gift. Neglect in helping other believers find their gift. These "grace gifts" are the primary channels through which our risen, living Lord continues His present-day ministry. Dr. J.I. Packer defines spiritual gifts as *"actualized powers for showing Christ forth."* Another describes them as, "*channels through which Christ performs His present work in our midst.*" I especially like that definition. Christ did not stop working in our midst 2,000 years ago when He ascended to the Father. *"So then, after the Lord had spoken to them, He was received up into heaven, and sat down at the right hand of God. And they went out and preached everywhere, the Lord working with them..."* I'm especially struck by the opening verse of Acts. "*The former account I made, O Theophilus, of all that Jesus began both to do and teach,*" (Acts 1:1.) Note the phrase "*began* to do and teach." In other words the teaching and doing ministry of our Lord did not end with the book of Luke ("the former account.") In the words of C.S. Lewis, "*Aslain is on the move.*" Jesus is still doing and teaching just as much as He was 2,000 years ago. Only now it's through His second earth-suit—you and me. And spiritual gifts are the primary outlets for His present, ongoing, supernatural doing and teaching.

It is a tragedy of monumental proportions for believers to go the entirety of their Christian lives and never know or utilize their spiritual gift(s). Even if they are faithful and serve in some sort of ministry. I fear that far too many believers think God is completely satisfied as long as they find a ministry and are faithful to it. After all, they're "serving the Lord," aren't they? What more could He want or expect?

I find it very intriguing and instructive that Paul reminds Timothy twice to play to his strength. "*Neglect not the gift that is in you,*" (I Tim. 4:14.) "*Therefore I remind you to fan into flame the gift of God which is in you,*" (II Tim. 1:6.) Why would Paul need to remind good-hearted, faithful Timothy to be sure and utilize his spiritual gift? Because ironically, one of the primary things that moves us away from properly utilizing our spiritual gift is ministry itself! **The tyranny of the urgent all too often trumps the giftedness of the saint.** There is no end to the number of things that need to be done in any worthwhile ministry. Pressing things, important things, need-to-be-done things. And all too often, sincere, wonderful-hearted believers have their hands so full of these good items that there is no room left for the best. Or to put it another way, we are so distracted by shooting our BB guns that we forget to fire our God-entrusted cannon, which is our main responsibility.

Certainly I realize that we don't only do things in ministry which are tied to our primary spiritual gifts. It has been well pointed out that somewhere in scripture all believers are called to do what some people have a spiritual gift for. In other words, not all of us have the gift of evangelism but we are all called to evangelize. Not all have the gift of mercy, but we are all responsible to show mercy. On and on it goes. But dangerous Christians refuse to allow their primary calling to become secondary and their secondary calling to become primary. Not that it's easy. But it is so, so important. Nothing will upgrade the quality and significance of one's life like this: doing the work of God through the gift of God by the Spirit of God for the glory of God. Get these four things to line up my friend, and you will be one extraordinarily dangerous Christian. And one extraordinarily satisfied human being as well.

Finally, **every genuine work of God is carefully crafted by God to spotlight God.** God alone, that is. The most important issue at stake in our work for God is not what it does for us or even what it does for others. It's what it does for God Himself. More specifically—His glory, His fame, and His reputation. It can't be said any more clear than in Peter's own words, *"As each one has received a gift, minister it to one another, as good stewards of the manifold grace of God. If anyone speaks, let him speak as the oracles of God. If anyone ministers, let him do it as with the ability which God supplies."* Then he adds, "*That in all things God may be glorified through Jesus Christ, to whom belong the glory and the dominion forever and ever. Amen," (*I Pet. 4:10, 11.)

It can't be more simple, more clear, or more radical. God supplies every believer with a unique spiritual gift. God then supplies every believer with spiritual ammunition to use that gift most effectively. "*If anyone speaks, let him speak as the oracles of God."* If we have a speaking gift, let us be sure our message is dripping with the naked, undiluted, unedited word of God. "*If anyone ministers, let him do it as with the ability which God supplies."* If we have a serving gift, let us be sure to serve in a strength that goes far beyond well-disciplined flesh. Let it be the supernatural strength God alone is capable of supplying. The result? This is so awesome. **The entirety of our ministry ("*that in all things*") is designed so that people are monumentally more impressed with God than us!** "*...That in all things God may be glorified.*" is the alpha and omega of everything in our lives, including ministry. No, especially ministry.

This is why Paul responded with such white hot, godly jealousy when the Corinthians began lining up behind the popular Christian leaders of the day. *"For when one says, 'I am of Paul,' and another, 'I am of Apollos,' are you not carnal? Who then is Paul, and who is Apollos, but ministers through whom you believed, as the Lord gave to each one? I planted, Apollos watered, but God gave the increase. So then neither he who plants is anything, nor he who waters, but God who gives the increase,"* (I Cor. 3:4-7.)

Every servant of God is, at best, only a temporary tool in the hand of our eternal God. As Charles Wesley wrote, *"God buries His workmen, but carries on His work."* I love the way Paul summarizes his entire take on ministry as God designed it. "*So then neither he who plants is anything, nor he who waters, but God who gives the increase."* Samuel Brengle, one of the early leaders of the Salvation Army, understood this well. One night he was introduced as the "great Dr. Brengle." That night he wrote in his diary:

"If I appear great in their eyes, the Lord is most graciously helping me to see how absolutely nothing I am without Him, and helping me to keep little in my own eyes. He does use me. But I am so concerned that He uses me and that it is not of me the work is done. The axe cannot boast of the trees it has cut down. It could do nothing but for the woodsman. He made it, he sharpened it, and he used it. The moment he throws it aside, it becomes only old iron. O, that I may never lose sight of this."

I love his thought, "*The axe cannot boast of the trees it has cut down. It could do nothing but for the woodsman."* Has God used you to cut down some spiritual trees to help build His eternal Kingdom? Great…enjoy it…and now get over it. He was using others before we got here and He'll use still others after we are gone. But right here, right now, we are His axe. And it is truly,

truly amazing the trees He can cut down with axes as blunt as ourselves. That just goes to show how astonishingly great a Woodsman He really is. But then again, that's the whole point, isn't it?

A man of prayer

"We give thanks to God always for you all, making mention of you in our prayers..." (I Thess. 1:2)

Dangerous Christians do not work alone. But they also do something else. They genuinely believe that **prayer is the front line of their spiritual attack and the single most important ministry activity in which they can engage.**

The first thing Paul reminds the Thessalonians of is the prayers that are being offered up on their behalf. Specific prayers...fiery prayers...frequent prayers. Most of all, Christ-scented prayers. I believe the reason that Paul mentions this first is that he believed so fiercely in the supremacy of prayer above all other ministry activities. J. Oswald Sanders writes,

"To read Paul's letters is to discover the supremely important place of prayer in the life of a spiritual leader. Nowhere does a leader expose the quality of his own spiritual life more clearly than in his prayers. We should be deeply grateful, therefore, for the unstudied self-revelation in the prayers that abound in the apostle's letters. He is at his best in his prayers. It is obvious that Paul did not regard prayer as supplemental, but as fundamental—not something to be added to his work, but the very matrix out of which his work was born...It was probably his prayer even more than his preaching that produced the kind of leaders we meet in his letters."

Paul's letters are bathed in references to the prayers he is making for those he has influenced. And those he has yet to influence. While certainly he prayed for his own needs and desires, these seem to take a backseat to the higher agenda that he possessed. Or perhaps better, that possessed him.

C. John Miller makes the distinction between "maintenance" praying and "frontline" praying. Maintenance praying is focused primarily upon our own needs, our own desires, our own family, our own job, etc. And this kind of praying is certainly important and a more than legitimate part of a full and healthy prayer life. *"Give us this day our daily bread and forgive us our trespasses," (*Mtt. 6:11, 12.) is mandated by our Lord Himself. Paul prayed for his thorn in the flesh to be removed and multiple other personal needs and items.

But frontline praying is what Paul specialized in. Our Lord described frontline praying as this, *"Our Father in heaven, hallowed be Your name. Your kingdom come. Your will be done on earth as it is in heaven," (*Mtt. 6:9, 10.) These words should be viewed more as a war cry than a Sunday morning platitude. It is the beseeching of God to wreak havoc in the kingdom of darkness, to send in ground troops to the cosmic battle taking place all around us, to strafe enemy territory with the gunfire of heaven. Just a short sampling of his prayers show unmistakably the frontline nature of his prayer life:

"Brothers, my heart's desire and prayer to God for them is that they may be saved," (Rom. 10:1.)

"For this reason I bow my knees before the Father, from whom every family in heaven and on earth is named, that according to the

riches of his glory he may grant you to be strengthened with power through his Spirit in your inner being, so that Christ may dwell in your hearts through faith—that you, being rooted and grounded in love, may have strength to comprehend with all the saints what is the breadth and length and height and depth, 19 and to know the love of Christ that surpasses knowledge, that you may be filled with all the fullness of God," (Eph. 4:14-19.)

"And it is my prayer that your love may abound more and more, with knowledge and all discernment, so that you may approve what is excellent, and so be pure and blameless for the day of Christ, filled with the fruit of righteousness that comes through Jesus Christ, to the glory and praise of God," (Phil. 1:9-11.)

"To this end we always pray for you, that our God may make you worthy of his calling and may fulfill every resolve for good and every work of faith by his power, so that the name of our Lord Jesus may be glorified in you, and you in him, according to the grace of our God and the Lord Jesus Christ," (II Thess. 1:11-13.)

One of the fascinating examples of the power of frontline praying comes from the life of J.O. Fraser. He joined China Inland Mission in 1908 and was assigned to minister both to Yunnan Province and Burma. He discovered after a while that the people in the group he was living with were not responding to the gospel or maturing nearly as quickly as the other people group he could only occasionally go to see. This seemed puzzling to him. Finally, he discovered the reason. Because he was actually living with the first group, he had subtly begun depending more on his preaching and discipling than on prayer. Because he wasn't able to be physically present with the other group, the Lisu, he prayed more fervently and frequently for them. And his frontline praying was bringing forth more fruit than his preaching and discipling. Ah, a great lesson for all of us!

Draw near to the genuinely dangerous Christians over the centuries and you will find, without exception, that frontline prayer was the foundation of all their Kingdom efforts.

"*Work, work, from morning until late at night. In fact, I have so much to do that I shall have to spend the first three hours in prayer.*" **Martin Luther**

"*The greatest thing anyone can do for God and man is pray. It is not the only thing; but it is the chief thing. The great people of the earth today are the people who pray. I do not mean those who talk about prayer; nor those who say they believe in prayer; nor yet those who can explain about prayer; but I mean those people who take time to pray.*" **S.D. Gordon**

"*The prayer power has never been tried to its full capacity…if we want to see mighty wonders of divine power and grace wrought in the place of weakness, failure, and disappointment, let us answer God's standing challenge, 'Call unto me, and I will answer thee, and show thee great and might things which thou knowest not.'*" **J. Hudson Taylor**

"*We lean to our own understanding, or we bank on service and do away with prayer, and consequently by succeeding in the external we fail in the eternal, because in the eternal we succeed only by prevailing prayer.*" **Oswald Chambers**

"The one concern of the Devil is to keep the saints from praying. He fears nothing from prayer-less studies, prayer-less work, prayer-less religion. He laughs at our toil, mocks at our wisdom, but trembles when we pray." **Samuel Chadwick**

Without a doubt, this commitment to and dependence upon prayer was one of the great, great strengths of the Moravian church. Perhaps the greatest. Professor Leslie Tarr writes:

During its first five years of existence the Herrnhut settlement showed few signs of spiritual power. By the beginning of 1727 the community of about three hundred people was wracked by dissension and bickering. An unlikely site for revival!

Zinzendorf and others, however, covenanted to prayer and labor for revival. On May 12 revival came. Christians were aglow with new life and power, dissension vanished, and unbelievers were converted. A spirit of prayer was immediately evident in the fellowship and continued throughout that "golden summer of 1727," as the Moravians came to designate the period. On August 27 of that year twenty-four men and twenty-four women covenanted to spend one hour each day in scheduled prayer.

Some others enlisted in the "hourly intercession."

'For over a hundred years the members of the Moravian Church all shared in the "hourly intercession." At home and abroad, on land and sea, this prayer watch ascended unceasingly to the Lord,' stated historian A. J. Lewis.

Did you catch that? For over 100 years, at least two Moravians were praying for an hour at a time, 24 hours a day, seven days a week! As a community they prayed 24 hours a day for over one hundred years. And their prayers were primarily frontline, interceding for their missionaries and for the advance of the gospel worldwide. Do you know what happened in church history from 1727-1827? The Great Awakening in America, the ministries of George Whitefield, Jonathan Edwards, and the Wesley brothers, just to name a few. Who knows but that this 100 year prayer watch was the single greatest weapon of that time period for inflicting damage to the kingdom of darkness? Certainly, it wouldn't be surprising.

Dangerous Christians follow in the footsteps of Paul. They are not sidetracked by drab religiosity, church politics, or lifeless rule keeping. They are men and women radically joined together in risk-taking, Christ-honoring community. They also believe to the core of their beings that aggressive, frontline prayer is their highest and most urgent calling in fighting the good fight. Let's look now at what they are fighting for.

Chapter 4

The Metrics of Success

...the world outside is not going to pay much attention to all the organized efforts of the Christian church. The one thing she will pay attention to is a body filled with this spirit and rejoicing. That is how Christianity conquered the ancient world.
—Dr. Martyn Lloyd Jones

I absolutely agree with Bill Hybels when he says, "*The local church is the hope of the world. There is nothing like the local church when it's working right. Its beauty is indescribable. Its power is breathtaking. Its potential is unlimited. It comforts the grieving and heals the broken in the context of community. It builds bridges to seekers and offers truth to the confused. It provides resources for those in need and opens its arms to the forgotten, the downtrodden, the disillusioned. It breaks the chains of addictions, frees the oppressed, and offers belonging to the marginalized of this world. Whatever the capacity for human suffering, the church has a greater capacity for healing and wholeness. Still to this day, the potential of the local church is almost more than I can grasp. No other organization on earth is like the church. Nothing even comes close.*"

I think Paul would have echoed a hearty amen to those words. No, I *know* he would have. Fact is, after being ambushed by Jesus, he spent the remainder of his life laser-focused on planting and strengthening local churches. He could have done a lot of things with his life. A lot of *Christian* things. But he chose under God to devote himself to peppering the known world of his day with local churches. And these local churches, though all of them imperfect to varying degrees, wreaked havoc on the gates of hell. These scattered, numerically small congregations (many scholars believe there were very few—if any—churches larger than 50 people for many years) ultimately brought Rome to her knees and the gospel to the masses. Hybels is right. At the end of the day, "*There is nothing like the local church when it's working right. Its beauty is indescribable. Its power is breathtaking. Its potential is unlimited.*"

The key to the whole thing of course is contained in his words "*when it's working right.*" The unavoidable question then is how do we know if it is working right? Or, to put it another way, what are the metrics of genuine, unquestionable, spiritual success? Metrics not established by today's church or contemporary culture, but by the word of God and fleshed out by the early church. Fortunately we don't have to look far to find these God-calibrated metrics. *"We give thanks to God always for you all…remembering without ceasing your work of faith, labor of love, and patience of hope in our Lord Jesus Christ in the sight of our God and Father,"* (I Thess. 1:3.)

As Paul sought to determine whether their ministry had been genuinely successful or not, he had an eagle eye for one thing above all else—*supernaturally changed lives.* Not just changed lives—many religions and ideologies are capable of that. No, this grace-soaked warrior refused to settle for anything less than men and women whose transformation could only be explained by a power unknown to everyone except Christ-followers. Far, far more important to him than numbers, baptisms, budgets, programs, etc., were walking flesh and blood monuments to the unrivaled, transforming power of the living God. He understood something we desperately need to be reminded of in our day. **Supernaturally changed lives make the gospel an issue like nothing else.** Period. In 1871, a roving, atheistic journalist named Henry Stanley was hired to go down into Africa to do a story on the famous explorer and medical missionary David Livingstone. After finding Livingstone ten months later, he went on to discover something more, as he himself recounts:

"For four months I lived with him in the same house or in the same boat or in the same tent, and I never found a fault in him. His gentleness never forsakes him. No harassing anxieties, distraction of mind, long separation from home and kindred, can make him complain. He thinks all will come out right at last; he has such faith in the goodness of Providence.

I went to Africa as prejudiced as the biggest atheist in London. But there came for me a long time of reflection. I saw this solitary old man there and asked myself, 'How on earth does he stop here—is he cracked, or what? What inspires him?' For months after we met I found myself wondering at the old man carrying out all that was said in the Bible—'Leave all things and follow Me.' But little by little his sympathy for others became contagious, my sympathy was aroused, seeing his piety, his gentleness, his zeal, his earnestness, and how he went about his business, I was converted by him, although he had not tried to do it."

Later Stanley wrote, "*It wasn't Livingstone's preaching that converted me, it was his living.*" Dangerous Christians lead with their lives—surprising lives, head scratching lives, curiosity arousing lives. Lives which can only be explained by another world, another power, and most of all—another Person. Lives like that of Ward Goodrich, the father of Bruce Goodrich.

I well remember an incident from the early 1980s while I was a college pastor in College Station, Texas. Incoming freshman Bruce Goodrich was being initiated into the corps of cadets at Texas A & M University. One early morning, he was forced to run until he dropped. Tragically, he never got up. Bruce Goodrich died at the very beginning of his first semester at A&M. The school, of course, prepared for the lawsuit which certainly the parents would bring against it. Unexpectedly, the lawsuit never came. But what did come was the following letter sent by Bruce's father to the administration, faculty, student body, and the corps of cadets. It was published in the school newspaper, *The Battalion,* and the city paper, *The Eagle.*

"I would like to take this opportunity to express the appreciation of my family for the great outpouring of concern and sympathy from Texas A & M University and the college community over the loss of our son Bruce. We were deeply touched by the tribute paid to him in The Battalion. We were particularly pleased to note that his Christian witness did not go unnoticed during his brief time on campus.

I hope it will be some comfort to know that we harbor no ill will in the matter. We know our God makes no mistakes. Bruce had an appointment with his Lord and is now secure in his celestial home.

When the question is asked, 'Why did this happen?' perhaps one answer will be, 'So that many will consider where they will spend eternity.'"

That letter rocked the A&M community and beyond. It preached more loudly than a thousand sermons ever could. Not that the thousand sermons don't have their place. But the best of sermons can still be quickly swept aside. Supernatural responses such as Mr. Goodrich's and his family make it more difficult to brush off the reality of a life-transforming God. Far, far more difficult.

John Wesley was once asked the reason behind the rapid growth of Methodism. He could have pointed to many factors—preaching the word, social good, strong organization, etc. Instead he pointed to one thing: *"our people die well."* A physician of that day remarked to Charles Wesley, *"Most people die for fear of dying; but, I never met with such people as yours. They are none of them afraid of death, but* [are] *calm, and patient, and resigned to the last."* It was the supernatural response of these Methodist believers to their impending home going which served as the primary catalyst for so many people taking the gospel seriously for the first time.

Ironically, it was this surprise element that was a very, very major factor in John Wesley's own conversion. And not surprisingly, it was members of the Moravian church who led the way. Early in his life, Wesley went to Georgia as a missionary. Though he was an ordained minister of the Anglican church and a missionary, he was not yet genuinely converted. On the ship over to Georgia, he found himself traveling with a group of Moravians. Here is his own account of the impact that the transformed Moravians had upon him:

Sunday, January 25, 1736 *"At seven I went to the Germans. I had long before observed the great seriousness of their behaviour. Of their humility they had given a continual proof, by performing those servile offices for the other passengers, which none of the English would undertake; for which they desired, and would receive no pay, saying, 'it was good for their proud hearts,' and 'their loving Saviour had done more for them.' And every day had given them occasion of showing a meekness which no injury could move. If they were pushed, struck, or thrown down, they rose again and went away; but no complaint was found in their mouth."*

Note the first thing that surprised Wesley—their extraordinary humility and their glad willingness to perform tasks on board which no one else was willing to do. And then refusing to be paid for them! Their reasons? *It was good for their proud hearts and their loving Saviour had done more for them.* Amazing! And then he recounts the next thing that blindsided him—their stunning calmness in the face of death.

"There was now an opportunity of trying whether they were delivered from the Spirit of fear, as well as from that of pride, anger, and revenge. In the midst of the psalm wherewith their service began, the sea broke over, split the main-sail in pieces, covered the ship, and poured in between the decks, as if the great deep had already swallowed us up. A terrible screaming began among the English. The Germans calmly sung on. I asked one of them afterwards, 'Was you not afraid?' He answered, 'I thank God, no.' I asked, 'But were

not your women and children afraid?' He replied, mildly, No; our women and children are not afraid to die.'"

Tuesday, February 24, 1736 *"Mr. Delamotte and I took up our lodging with the Germans (the Moravians). We had now an opportunity, day by day, of observing their whole behaviour. For we were in one room with them from morning to night, unless for the little time I spent in walking. They were always employed, always cheerful themselves, and in good humour with one another; they had put away all anger and strife, and wrath, and bitterness, and clamour, and evil-speaking; they walked worthy of the vocation wherewith they were called, and adorned the Gospel of our Lord in all things."*

Ultimately, God was to use a Moravian leader named Peter Boehler to lead John to Christ. But it was the lifestyle of the Moravians and their response to adversity which caused Wesley to begin reexamining his own spirituality. So much so that he would write in his journal on his journey back to England, *"I went to America to convert the Indians, but oh, who shall convert me? I have a fair summer religion. I can talk well; nay, and I believe myself, when no danger is near. But let death look me in the face, and my spirit is troubled. Nor can I say, 'to die is gain.' I have a sort of fear that when I have spun my last thread I shall perish on the shore. I have learned that I who went to America to convert others was not converted myself."* May I say it again? Supernaturally-changed lives make the gospel an issue like nothing else. In Wesley's day…and ours.

What were the things Paul looked for as the clearest evidence of supernatural change, the surest metrics of spiritual success? The answer may well surprise you, for they are few in number and are almost always remarkably absent on the punch list which most ministries use for their measurement of ministry success. You won't often find these highlighted in most of today's church growth literature. On the other hand, Paul was a fanatic about seeing these as the very pillars of every church he planted. Very simply, they are *faith*, *hope,* and *love.*

"...Remembering without ceasing your work of *faith*, labor of *love*, and patience of *hope* in our Lord Jesus Christ in the sight of our God and Father," (I Thess. 1:3.)

"But let us who are of the day be sober, putting on the breastplate of *faith* and *love*, and as a helmet the *hope* of salvation," (I Thess. 5:8.)

"Because your *faith* grows exceedingly, and the *love* of every one of you all abounds toward each other, so that we ourselves boast of you among the churches of God for your patience," (II Thess. 1:3, 4.) Note: *Hope* is not mentioned because this was what he was trying to revive in the epistle.

"...Since we heard of your *faith* in Christ Jesus and of your *love* for all the saints; because of the *hope* which is laid up for you in heaven," (Col. 1:4, 5.)

"And now abide *faith*, *hope*, *love*, these three; but the greatest of these is love," (I Cor. 13:13.)

Even the writer of Hebrews was looking for these same three pillars. "...Let us draw near with a true heart in full assurance of *faith*, having our hearts sprinkled from an evil conscience and our bodies washed with pure water. Let us hold fast the confession of our *hope* without wavering, for He who promised is faithful. And let us consider one another in order to stir up *love* and good works," (Heb. 10:22-24.)

Don't pass by Paul's statement, "*And now abide faith, hope, love, these three*," too quickly. The fact that he adds the phrase "*these three*" demonstrates beyond question that he saw these three as the trinity of true spirituality and ministry success. This is a complete and monumental game changer. **In every church he planted, Paul looked for these three virtues above everything else to measure the spiritual vitality and success of that ministry.** Please, please let that sink in. How many churches and ministries do you know that are laser focused on faith, hope, and love as paramount to their true success? I submit...not enough. Not nearly enough. Neither today nor historically.

But was he not interested in numbers...in conversions...in giving...in growth...etc.? Certainly he was interested in these things, but never controlled by them. He understood that if these three vital virtues were in place, the rest would follow suit in God's timing. He would get evangelism, discipleship, growth, ministry, etc., when these three pillars were firmly set in place. As C.S. Lewis put it so well, *"Put first things first and you get second things thrown in. Put second things first and you lose both first and second."* If one has the fire, then one inevitably gets the light and warmth. Go for the jugular and you get the whole person. But as I mentioned, too few churches and ministries throughout history or even today have made these metrics their top priority. But when they have, typically God's blessing on that church or ministry has been unmistakably evident.

What then did Paul mean by *"your work of faith, labor of love, and patience of hope?"* Or, as the NIV translates, *"Your work produced by faith, your labor prompted by love, and your endurance inspired by hope."* Fortunately Paul describes very specifically what he meant by each of these later in this same chapter. *"For they themselves declare concerning us what manner of entry we had to you, and how you turned to God from idols to serve the living and true God, and to wait for His Son from heaven," (*I Thess. 1:9, 10.)

The "*work of faith*" was "*how you turned to God from idols.*" The "*labor of love*" was "*to serve the living and true God.*" And the "*patience of hope*" was "*to wait for His Son from heaven.*" Let's look at each of these and the importance they hold for vital, dynamic, head-turning Christianity. Game changers have three vital characteristics in common. They are:

Men and women supremely satisfied in the person of God.

This is the "*work of faith.*" It's interesting to note that he doesn't say "*how that you turned from idols to God,*" but "*how that you turned to God from idols.*" In a word, they "traded up." When they heard of the "*true and living God,*" they readily emptied their hands of their false and dead gods in order to take hold of the God Who astronomically trumped everything their former gods had to offer. While certainly this refers to their initial conversion, no doubt it also goes beyond that first act of turning to an ongoing lifestyle of being supremely satisfied in Christ and Christ alone.

Nothing more clearly demonstrates the utter trustworthiness and supreme awesomeness of our God than the paucity

of secondary gods in our lives. When men and women are supremely satisfied with the true and living God, then they will follow in the footsteps of Ephraim. *"Ephraim shall say, 'What have I to do anymore with idols?' I have heard and observed Him. I am like a green cypress tree; your fruit is found in Me,'"* (Hosea 14:8.) When men and women have traded up to the degree that they say to themselves, *"What have I to do anymore with idols?"* their God-drenched life preaches more loudly than a thousand sermons. As John Piper puts it so well, *"God is most glorified in us when we are most satisfied in Him."* Paul believed this to the core of his being and proclaimed it to the end of his days. No wonder he admonishes, *"Therefore, my beloved, flee from idolatry,"* (I Cor. 10:14.) Or that John concludes his letter on the supernatural, exquisite joy of ever deepening intimacy with God by writing, "*Little children, keep yourselves from idols. Amen*," (I Jn. 5:21.) A.W. Tozer puts it so well, *"God formed us for His pleasure, and so formed us that we as well as He can in divine communion enjoy the sweet and mysterious mingling of kindred personalities. He meant us to see Him and live with Him and draw our life from His smile."*

I love his phrase, "*...Draw our life from His smile*." The grave danger of idols is that they seduce us into exchanging His smile for their handshake. And that is a bad trade indeed. So what exactly are today's idols? Like every generation, there is a wide assortment: money, cars, homes, jobs, etc. They can be highly respectable idols such as children, spouse, ministry, etc. Or they can be baser idols such as drugs, pornography, etc. People's idols can vary dramatically from person to person, and one man's idol may simply be another man's legitimate enjoyment. Let me suggest two questions which I think help identify the idols or potential idols in our lives.

What things, persons, or activities save me from the terror of having to trust God alone? As C.S. Lewis noted, our great problem in life is not trusting God; it is trusting God *alone.* Trusting God is no problem as long as we have secondary, pinch-hitting gods safely kept in reserve in the event that He does not come through. But there can easily arise a sense of panic deep within when we are put in the position where no other Provider for our material, physical, emotional, or relational welfare exists except the unseen and often unfelt God. Tim Keller puts it well. *"An idol is whatever you look at and say, in your heart of hearts, 'If I have that, then I'll feel my life has meaning, then I'll know I have value, then I'll feel significant and secure.'... If anything in life becomes more fundamental than God to your happiness, meaning in life, and identity, then it is an idol."* In other words, idolatry occurs when we cross over from *desiring* something for our happiness to *requiring* that same thing for our happiness.

When believers have the courage to empty their hands of reserve gods and fill their hands with only the true and living God, the world takes notice. In A.D. 404 John Chrysostom was brought in before the Roman emperor Arcadius. The emperor threatened him with banishment if he remained a Christian.

Chrysostom responded, *"You cannot banish me, for this world is my Father's house."*

"But I will kill you," said the emperor.

"No, you cannot, for my life is hid with Christ in God," said Chrysostom.

"I will take away your treasures."

"No, you cannot, for my treasure is in heaven and my heart is there."

"But I will drive you away from your friends and you will have no one left."

"No, you cannot, for I have a friend in heaven from whom you cannot separate me. I defy you, for there is nothing you can do to harm me."

No wonder the early Christians were taken seriously by the unbelievers around them!

What things, persons, or activities cause me to become bored with God? The human heart is incapable of carrying on two true love affairs at the same time. Either our love affair with God will cause our heart to become increasingly bored with the gods of this world, or our love affair with the gods of this world will cause our heart to become increasingly bored with God. No way around it. God's description of idolatrous Israel was this: *"...Ephraim is a cake unturned," (*Hosea 7:8.) The cake He was referring to was very much like today's tortilla. God is saying that

His people are hot to the point of being burnt on the earthward side, but cold on the heavenward side. Or as John puts it, *"Do not love the world or the things in the world. If anyone loves the world, the love of the Father is not in him,"* (I Jn. 2:15.) John is not saying that we cannot *enjoy* the things of the world, for as Paul states, "*God...gives us richly all things to enjoy,*" (I Tim. 6:17.) The problem arises when we begin holding onto these things too tightly, when the roots of our heart make their way down so deeply into them that God becomes a distant, estranged Lover. As Jonathan Edwards wrote, "*The enjoyment of God is the only happiness with which our souls can be satisfied...Fathers and mothers, husbands, wives, or children, or the company of earthly friends, are but shadows; but God is the substance. These are but scattered beams, but God is the sun. These are but streams. But God is the ocean.*"

The very first metric of ministry success in Paul's evaluation was that his converts were growing deeper and deeper in their white hot love affair with Jesus Christ. That subtle idols were being routinely discarded in favor of tasting more fully the delights of Trinitarian communion. And this God-enamored life tended to be the rule rather than the exception in the early church. Around 249, Cyprian wrote these words to his friend Donatus:

"Donatus, this is a cheerful world indeed as I see it from my fair garden, under the shadow of my vines. But if I could ascend some high mountain, and look out over the wide lands, you know very well that I should see: brigands on the highways, pirates on the seas, armies fighting, cities burning, in the amphitheaters men murdered to please applauding crowds, selfishness and cruelty and misery and

despair under all roofs. It is a bad world, Donatus, an incredibly bad world. But I have discovered in the midst of it a company of quiet and holy people who have learned a great secret. They have found a joy which is a thousand times better than any of the pleasures of our sinful life. They are despised and persecuted, but they care not: they are masters of their souls. They have overcome the world. These people, Donatus, are the Christians,—and I am one of them."

Cyprian was later beheaded for his faith. But before then, he was mightily used by God to touch many people's lives. And the foundation of it all was "*a joy which is a thousand times better,*" a joy that he discovered in being supremely satisfied in Christ.

Likewise, the Moravians exemplified marvelously this first characteristic of being supremely satisfied in God. They were known in their day as "God's happy people." In fact if you look at the portraits of the early Moravians you can see unmistakable evidence of supernatural joy and peace on their countenances. The entire movement was profoundly influenced by Zinzendorf's own love of Christ. The sentence that probably best summarized his life was his own: *"I have but one passion—it is He, it is He alone."*

Men and women joyously abandoned to the work of God.

Out of the overflow of being supremely satisfied in the person of God, they launched forth in joyous abandonment to fulfilling the work of God. As the passage records, their "*labor of love*" was "*to serve the living and true God.*"

I love, but love the fact that serving God is described here as "*labor of love,*" or even better, "*labor prompted by love.*" These were anything but grim-faced, dutiful servants joylessly carrying out their Christian responsibilities. Or to put it another way, they were not *resigned* to the will of God but were *abandoned* to it. And that difference makes all the difference. As Michael Green notes, "*One of the most notable impressions the literature of the first and second century made upon me as I wrote this book was the sheer passion of these early Christians. They were passionately convinced of the truth of the gospel. They were persuaded that men and women were lost without it. They shared in God's own love, poured out on a needy world. They paid heed to Christ's Great Commission. They sought to interpenetrate society with the gospel which had so profound an effect upon them.*"

Paul himself wonderfully modeled this joy and abandonment in doing God's will. *"But none of these things move me, neither count I my life dear unto myself, so that I might finish my course with joy, and the ministry, which I have received of the Lord Jesus, to testify the gospel of the grace of God," (*Acts 20:24.) *"Yes, and if I am being poured out as a drink offering on the sacrifice and service of your faith, I am glad and rejoice with you all,"* (Phil. 2:17.) For Paul, "joy" and "obedience" were not incompatible; they were in fact the best of friends. And a host of saints throughout the church age would echo a hearty amen to that:

"The sheer joy of it all comes back. Gladly would I do it all over again." Samuel Zwemer, describing his 23 years of ministry in Bahrain which were marked by great difficulties and sorrows, as well as very little visible fruit.

"For my own part, I have never ceased to rejoice that God has appointed me to such an office. People talk of the sacrifice I have made in spending so much of my life in Africa. . . . Is that a

sacrifice which brings its own blest reward in healthful activity, the consciousness of doing good, peace of mind, and a bright hope of a glorious destiny hereafter? Away with the word in such a view, and with such a thought! It is emphatically no sacrifice. Say rather it is a privilege. Anxiety, sickness, suffering, or danger, now and then, with a foregoing of the common conveniences and charities of this life, may make us pause, and cause the spirit to waver, and the soul to sink; but let this only be for a moment. All these are nothing when compared with the glory which shall be revealed in and for us. I never made a sacrifice," David Livingstone speaking to the students at Cambridge University.

John Piper puts it well, *"...God's deepest purpose for the world is to fill it with reverberations of his glory in the lives of a new humanity, ransomed from every people, tribe, tongue, and nation (Rev 5:9.) But the glory of God does not reflect brightly in the hearts of men and women when they cower unwillingly in submission to his authority or when they obey in servile fear or when there is no gladness in response to the glory of their King...The only submission that fully reflects the worth and glory of the King is glad submission."* Elsewhere he writes, *"No gladness in the subject, no glory to the King."* I love that!

It's interesting to note that the word used here for "*labor*" is a different word than the word for "*work*" previously used concerning faith. This particular word always carries with it the connotation of working to the point of weariness. It is the very word used in Jn. 4:6 of Christ being "*wearied*" at Jacob's well. The point is simply this: in ministry it costs to count. No way around it. It costs in terms of physical exhaustion. It costs in terms of emotional draining. It costs in terms of spiritual exertion. It costs in terms of lost sleep, late nights, and way too early meetings. It costs in terms of being misunderstood, maligned, and neglected. It costs in terms of showing up, showing up, showing up...with little to no visible fruit in terms of responsiveness. If love for a Person is not the primary driving force behind our service, it will only be a matter of time before we either throw in the towel or degenerate into modern day Pharisees.

In what ways did these early saints "*serve the living and true God?*" First and foremost it was by the extraordinary ways they loved one another. Tertullian writes:

"But it is mainly the deeds of a love so noble that lead many to put a brand upon us. See, they say, how they love one another, for they themselves are animated by mutual hatred. See, they say about us, how they are ready even to die for one another, for they themselves would sooner kill."

Justin Martyr records:

"We who used to value the acquisition of wealth and possessions more than anything else now bring what we have into a common fund and share it with anyone who needs it. We used to hate and destroy one another and refused to associate with people of another race or country. Now, because of Christ, we live together with such people and pray for our enemies."

Without a doubt it was the visible, God-stained love flowing back and forth among fellow believers which arrested the attention of outsiders more than any other single thing.

Beyond this, they gladly served their God by utilizing their spiritual gifts, sharing the gospel with those willing to listen, discipling fellow believers, taking in the homeless, caring for the sick, and a plethora of other Christ-compelled activities. Their lives and service for God are best summed up in the words of Paul, *"For the love of Christ constrains us,"* (II Cor. 5:14.)

Dangerous Christians *"serve the living and true God"* not *for* God's blessings but *because* of God's blessings. In other words, what thrusts them forward to make the living God visible on the playing field of life is the sheer gratitude and unbridled joy engendered by the wide-eyed wonder of all that the gospel has done for them. And continues to do. Gypsy Smith circled the globe for almost 70 years, influencing the lives of literally millions of people for the gospel. Toward the end of his life he was asked what kept him going all those years. His answer? *"I never lost the wonder of it all."* What a great way to put it! Game changers are game changers first and foremost because they manage to never lose the magic, the mystery, and especially the wonder of the gospel. And because of this, their service for God is scented and perfumed with a gratitude and joy which those around cannot miss.

This too, was one of the great characteristics of the early Moravian church, especially their missionaries. I've already mentioned the first two missionaries who went to the West Indies intending to sell themselves into slavery so they could reach the slaves there. Their joyous abandonment and zeal is best summarized by Robert Murray McCheyne, the Scottish pastor, as he was speaking to his congregation about the need for ministry to lepers:

"But you will ask, who cares for the souls of the hapless inmates? Who will venture to enter in at this dreadful gate, never to return again? Who will forsake father and mother, houses and land, to carry the message of a Saviour to these poor lepers? Two Moravian missionaries, impelled by a divine love for souls, have chosen the lazarhouse as their field of labor. They entered it never to come out again; and I am told that as soon as these die, other Moravians are quite ready to fill their place. Ah! my dear friends, may we not blush, and be ashamed before God, that we, redeemed with the same blood, and taught by the same Spirit, should yet be so unlike these men in vehement, heart-consuming love to Jesus and the souls of men?" I love his last description, *vehement, heart-consuming love to Jesus and the souls of men.* Hard to improve on that!

Men and women radiantly anticipating the return of Christ

These men and women were first and foremost supremely satisfied in God. This naturally issued forth into their joyous abandonment to His calling on their lives. But there was still one thing needed for these saints to maximize all their God-given potential. That final commodity, so crucial to their ongoing influence, is described by Paul as "*patience of hope.*" Without it, they would never become all that God had designed them to be. And of course, neither will we.

It is difficult to overstate how important patience, endurance, and perseverance are in becoming a dangerous Christian. It is the super-glue of spiritual success and by it so many of God's servants have achieved more than any thought possible. William

Carey translated the Bible into over 40 different Indian dialects from 1793 to 1834. Though he never graduated from even high school, Carey became one of the greatest linguists the world has ever known. This Englishman overcame tremendous obstacles and setbacks during his years in India. One of his children died, his wife became mentally ill, death threats were made against him, and his home and much of his translation work were destroyed in a great fire. He ministered for seven years before he saw his first convert. Shortly before he died, he gave out his secret for success to his sister, Eunice:

"If, after my removal, anyone should think it worth his while to write my life, I will give you a criterion by which you may judge its correctness. If he will give me credit for being a plodder, he will describe me justly. Anything beyond this will be too much. I can plod. I can persevere in any definite pursuit. To this I owe everything."

A host of dangerous Christians would echo the same sentiment as Carey. *"I can plod. I can persevere in any definite pursuit. To this I owe everything."* How then does one keep plodding? The answer is given to us in word—patience. The word for "patience" is one of the great words of the New Testament. It literally means to "remain or abide under." It was used to describe a plant which was crushed underfoot but kept rising back up again. New Testament scholar William Barclay writes of this word, *"It is not the patience which can sit down and bow its head and let things descend upon it and passively endure until the storm is past. . . . It is the spirit which can bear things, not simply with resignation, but with blazing hope; it is . . . the spirit which bears things because it knows that these things are leading to a goal of glory; it is not the patience which grimly waits for the end, but the patience which radiantly hopes for the dawn."* I love his phrase, *it is the spirit which can bear things, not simply with resignation, but with blazing hope.* In other words, it was not the stiff upper lip of the stoic but the supernaturally enabled resilience of the Christ-lover. I like to define it as "God-honoring resilience."

This truly was one of the things that most stunned unbelievers watching the early Christians. Routinely Christ-followers would go their deaths singing. Though often treated with extreme cruelty and blatant injustice, they refused to retaliate. Their response to ruthless authorities was to pray for them and honor them for their position of authority.

One of the greatest examples of how early believers faced death for their faith is that of two women, Perpetua and Felicity, who were believed to have died in 203 AD. Vibia Perpetua was a married noblewoman, said to have been 22 years old at the time of her death, and mother of an infant she was nursing. Felicity, a slave imprisoned with her and pregnant at the time, was martyred with her. As they approached their martyrdom, an eyewitness recounted:

"The day of their victory (i.e. martyrdom) *dawned, and they marched from the prison to the amphitheater joyfully as though they were going to heaven, with calm faces, trembling, if at all, with joy rather than fear. Perpetua went along with shining countenance and calm step, as the beloved of God, as a wife of Christ, putting down everyone's stare by her own intense gaze. With them also was Felicitas, glad that she had safely given birth so that now she could fight the beasts…*

They were then led up to the gates and the men were forced to put on the robes of priests of Saturn, the women the dress of the priestesses of Ceres. But the noble Perpetua strenuously resisted this to the end.

'We came to this of our own free will, that our freedom should not be violated. We agreed to pledge our lives provided that we would do no such thing. You agreed with us to do this.'

Even injustice recognized justice. The military tribune agreed. They were to be brought into the arena just as they were. Perpetua then began to sing a psalm...

At this the crowds became enraged and demanded that they be scourged before a line of gladiators. And they rejoiced at this that they had obtained a share in the Lord's sufferings."

These two women along with several men laid down their lives in blood that day; but their supernatural responses no doubt lingered in the minds of those watching for a long time.

What was it that provided the early saints with the hope that inspired such godly endurance? This is what is particularly fascinating...and important. The hope was found in radiant anticipation, "*to wait for His Son from heaven*." Nowhere will you find Paul or the other writers of the New Testament encouraging, "Hang in there, your circumstances will get better." Or, "Be patient, your blessing is right around the corner." They didn't even focus that much on death as the great deliverer from earth's troubles and woes. Paul (as well as the other New Testament authors) had one central focal point that they relentlessly pushed their readers to rivet their hopes upon. It was this: Jesus would physically return to this earth, and when this happened

He would make everything right. In fact, He would not only make things right, He would make them unfathomably and indescribably perfect. And this "blessed hope," as it was called, could happen at any moment…and certainly within their lifetime. The word "*hope*" was not referring to wishful thinking as we often use it (i.e. I hope our team will win the game), but confident expectation of certain fulfillment.

The early Christians fully expected to see Jesus before they saw death. They didn't measure the end of their earthly sojourn by when they stopped breathing but by when Jesus would split the skies. Alexander Maclaren put it so well, *"The primitive church thought more about the second coming of Jesus Christ than about death or about heaven. The early Christians were looking not for a cleft in the ground called a grave, but for a cleavage in the sky called Glory. They were watching not for the 'undertaker' but for the 'Uppertaker.'"*

Historically skeptics inside and outside of the church have not been shy to point out how wrong these early Christians were in their timetable for Christ's return. What they haven't been so quick to acknowledge is that this perspective was unquestionably a key factor in the unrivaled vitality and influence of the church during the first three centuries. Virtually all these early believers lived under the spell and sway of Christ's immediate return. This conviction rearranged their priorities, profoundly influenced their pursuits, and provided the renewed hope which enabled fatigued radicals to press on through one more day of battle. We would do well to follow in their footsteps. We would do even better to live our lives with their same awareness of Christ's ever present possibility of returning at any moment.

And so here we have it. Paul evaluated the success of his ministry by changed lives. *Supernaturally* changed lives. More specifically, men and women who were supremely satisfied in the Person of God, joyously abandoned to the work of God, and radiantly anticipating the return of Christ. These are the big three. These are the indispensable three. These are the indisputable, game changer three.

Paul understood that if he got these three, he would get everything else essential for kingdom advance. This is exactly why he so, so valued these three godly qualities. This is why he wrote to the Thessalonians, *"remembering without ceasing your work of faith, labor of love, and patience of hope in our Lord Jesus Christ."* Why doesn't he simply say, "*Remembering your work of faith*?" Why does he add the words, "*without ceasing?*" Because he esteemed faith, hope, and love so highly that they were foremost in his mind when he thought of the Thessalonians and their spiritual progress. Then look at this. What caused his heart to leap when he heard how the Thessalonians were doing? *"But now that Timothy has come to us from you, and brought us good news of your faith and love,"* (I Thess. 3:6.) In fact the word he uses here for "*good news*" is exactly the same word translated "*gospel*" elsewhere. The reason he doesn't mention "*hope*" is that it was waning because of the death of some of the saints and he writes to correct their understanding and revive their hope.

Supernaturally changed lives stained by faith, hope, and love. Pretty simple, really. But also extraordinarily powerful.

Paul was not primarily focused upon church structure or organization. But he was an absolute fanatic about life change made possible only by the Spirit of God. My, how far we have veered since Paul's day! On the whole, today's church has become far more a well-structured *organization* than a living, breathing, reproducing *organism.*

How many churches and Christian organizations today use faith, hope, and love as their primary metrics for spiritual progress? I fear too few. And candidly, for much of my ministry I didn't either. I only wish I had seen these things earlier.

Many, if not most ministries and churches today are opting for immediately measurable, tangible, metrics. According to renowned church growth expert George Barna, here are the top five metrics primarily used today:

1. Attendance (number of people)
2. Giving (number of dollars)
3. Programs (number of budgeted activities)
4. Staff (number of persons on payroll)
5. Square Footage (number of facilities)

Barna then makes this observation, *"Now all of those things are good measures, except for one tiny fact: Jesus didn't die for any of them."* So true! **One of the greatest impact neutralizers in the church today is unrecognized distraction.** Because so much of our firepower is being directed toward bigger buildings, more programs, better events, etc.; we have precious little firepower left to spend on what matters most—supernaturally changed lives for God's glory.

C.S. Lewis well understood all this well and it caused him to write one of the great descriptions of what church is to be about. *"It is easy to think that the Church has a lot of different objects—education, building, missions, holding services...the Church exists for nothing else but to draw men into Christ, to make them little Christs. If they are not doing that, all the cathedrals, clergy, missions, sermons, even the Bible itself, are simply a waste of time. God became Man for no other purpose."*

Finally, it must not be overlooked that one of the foremost strengths of the early church was the utter absence of a clergy/laity distinction. For the most part, everyone was "all in." Paul begins this epistle saying, *"We thank God always* ***for all of you*** (emphasis mine)." He then goes on to commend **all** the Thessalonian saints for their *"work of faith, labor of love, and patience of hope."* Michael Green writes, *"There was no distinction in the early church between full time ministers and laymen in this responsibility to spread the gospel by every means possible, there was equally no distinction between the sexes in the matter. It was axiomatic that every Christian was called to be a witness to Christ, not only by life but lip."* Elsewhere he writes, *"The very disciples themselves were, significantly, laymen, devoid of formal theological training. Christianity was from its inception a lay movement, and so it continued for a remarkably long time."* In the early days there were church **leaders** (elders, deacons, etc.) but no church **professionals**. But we will save this vital discussion for another chapter. For now, we want to continue by seeing what caused Paul, Silas, and Timothy to have such astonishing and life-transforming impact upon these Thessalonians. Let's take a look...

Chapter 5

A Three–Pronged Attack

Make me Thy fuel, O Flame of God.
—Amy Carmichael

When Joshua took possession of the Promised Land, he did so with a three- pronged attack. He first took control of the central region of the land, then the southern, and finally the northern territory. To this day, it is considered one of the most brilliant tactical assaults ever devised in military history. This is not that surprising, since this three-pronged attack was devised by God and not Joshua. Joshua and the Israelites were simply following God into battle and depending upon Him to secure victories through them which they could never have done on their own.

This is exactly what God did thousands of years later with Paul, Silas, and Timothy as they invaded territory still fully controlled by the gates of hell. They followed the Spirit of God into Thessalonica with a message which wholly originated from God. They did so with a burning enthusiasm, a holy zeal, a fiery passion wholly engendered by the Holy Spirit. And they lived lives which were so remarkably surprising and compelling that the only possible explanation was supernatural empowerment. This was their three-pronged attack. These are the exact three things which Paul points out to the Thessalonians as the reason for their deep spiritual impact upon these men and women. And these same three things—whenever given the chance—are still mighty gate busters and game changers, dreaded by the forces of darkness. They are described in I Thess. 1:5:

"For our gospel did not come to you in word alone, but also in power, and in the Holy Spirit and in much assurance, as you know what kind of men we were among you for your sake."

In short, they brought three mighty weapons into Thessalonica—*the word of God, the fire of God, and the glory of God.* Or to put it another way, the word of God, holy passion, and surprising lives.

First weapon of attack—the word of God. *"For our gospel did not come to you in word alone…"* While their presentation of the gospel "*did not come to you in word alone,*" it still did very much come in word. The word of God, that is. Paul makes that unmistakably clear in the very next verse, *"And you became followers of us and of the Lord, having received the word in much affliction, with joy of the Holy Spirit,"* (I Thess. 1:6.) A little later he will write concerning this exact same thing, *"For this reason we also thank God without ceasing, because when you received the word of God which you heard from us, you welcomed it not as the word of men, but as it is in truth, the word of God, which also effectively works in you who believe," (*I Thess. 2:13.)

One of the things that so clearly marked the ministry of Paul and that of believers in the early years of the church was nothing short of a fanaticism for getting the naked, unedited, undiluted word of God out into circulation within their natural spheres of influence. They understood that when people get face to face with the word of God in meaningful ways, lives get turned upside down. You see this commitment to getting the word out throughout the book of Acts:

"Then the word of God spread, and the number of the disciples multiplied greatly in Jerusalem, and a great many of the priests were obedient to the faith." Acts 6:7

"Therefore those who were scattered went everywhere preaching the word." Acts 8:4

"And when they arrived in Salamis, they preached the word of God in the synagogues of the Jews." Acts 13:5

On and on it goes. These men and women believed with every fiber of their beings that they had absolutely nothing more important to say to their fellow man than what God had already said. They recognized that every time they uttered or passed along the unvarnished, actual word of God, they were tossing out hand grenades—spiritual hand grenades whose explosion could set men and women free from the shackles of Satan's captivity.

In my years of ministry I have seen this time after time after time after time. When people are willing to seriously engage the scriptures for themselves, not simply read about the scriptures in commentaries or Christian books, one of two things happens. Either their lives begin to change or they stop interacting with the scripture and pull back. Which is exactly the parable of the soils.

The early believers pushed forward the word of God both *spontaneously* and *intentionally*. And they did so through various means. One was open air preaching as we see at times throughout the book of Acts. Note especially Stephen's message in Acts 7:1-53 and the tremendous amount of quoted scripture throughout his message. But open air preaching was undoubtedly the very least used method of dispensing God's word. Green writes, *"When we think of evangelistic methods today, preaching in a church building or perhaps a great area readily comes to mind. We must, of course, rid ourselves of all such preconceptions when thinking of evangelism by the early Christians. They knew nothing of set addresses following certain homiletical patterns within the four walls of a church. Indeed, for more than 150 years they possessed no church buildings, and there was the greatest variety in the type and content of Christian evangelistic preaching."*

The vast majority of transferring the word of God to the people of their day was the informal, spontaneous interactions of believers with their friends, acquaintances, and chance encounters. Walter Oetting writes:

"When the early Christians themselves recount how they learned of the Gospel, they usually confess their faith was the result of casual contact with that 'way of life'... Gregory came to study in Caesarea and happened to find a Christian teacher. Minucius Felix described how Octavius told Caecilius about his Christianity in casual conversation. Justin Martyr was accosted by an old man along the seashore who explained the Old Testament to him. Justin recalled that he was converted to the faith when he saw people willing to die for it in the area. The pagan Celsus scoffed at the workers in wool and leather, the rustic and ignorant persons who spread Christianity. The work was not by people who called themselves missionaries, but by rank-and-file members."

Along these same lines, Michael Green notes, *"It would be a gross mistake to suppose that the apostles sat down and worked out a plan of campaign: the spread of Christianity was, as we have seen, largely accomplished by informal missionaries, and must have been to a large extent haphazard and spontaneous."*

I'm particularly intrigued with his words *haphazard and spontaneous*. As we read the New Testament, one cannot help but sense this. **One of the things that characterized the early church was "minimal organization, maximum organism."** While there were some organized roles within local churches, such as elders, deacons, and deaconesses, there were far less than we might have thought. The early believers seem remarkably unconcerned about church structure, organization, and campaign strategies. The reason was that they were so busy getting the good news out, mostly in their natural spheres of influence, that they didn't have time to get sidetracked on church politics and structure. They had bigger fish to fry.

Not surprisingly, we find this same characteristic among the Moravians. Dr. Ryoo writes, *"It is almost impossible to maintain that before sending out missionaries the Moravian Church deliberately established specific missions strategies on how to preach the gospel or on how to start churches. Their strategy did not derive from an elaborate plan, but it was an accumulated lesson which the missionaries learned when they were ministering on the field. As they pursued the ideal of the apostles of Jesus in the early church, they tried to follow the model employed in the New Testament."*

One of the most effective methods for spreading God's word came through the use of homes. We see them referred to over and over in the New Testament. Again, Green writes, *"One of the most important methods of spreading the gospel in antiquity was by the use of homes. It had positive advantages: the comparatively small numbers involved made real interchange of views and informed discussion among the participants possible; there was no artificial isolation of a preacher from his hearers; there was no temptation for either the speaker or the heckler to 'play the gallery' as there was in a public place or open-air meeting."*

In fact, as one studies the history of revivals we find the very same thing. Home gatherings always seemed to play a major role in times of spiritual awakening and renewal. And most often, they were viewed contemptuously by the formal church.

While the word of God was relayed informally and spontaneously, it was also passed on *intentionally*. As Paul reminds Timothy, *"And the things that you have heard from me among many witnesses, commit these to faithful men who will be able to teach others also,"* (II Tim. 2:2.) We see here that Paul intentionally entrusted Timothy with the word of God and now Timothy is to intentionally do the same to others, who are to turn around and entrust it to still others. This is often referred to as the process of disciple making, which was normative Christianity in the early years. And in the last 70 years I believe we have seen a significant revival of this great undertaking, though certainly there is much room for continued growth.

What is particularly striking and unspeakably important is the identity of these early disciple makers. They were the everyday rank and file believers taken from every strata of society. And for the most part, they discipled those within in their own natural sphere of influence. In other words, tax collectors discipled tax collectors, older women mentored younger women, fishermen trained fishermen, soldiers influenced soldiers, etc. Milton L. Rudnick writes, *"During these early centuries Christianity grew so rapidly that the chief agents of growth were, not the leaders of the church nor professional evangelists, but rather ordinary believers…"* Discipleship was always designed to be the work of all believers, not to be the responsibility or privilege of a select, specially trained group of elite saints. Once passing along the word of God began to be primarily reserved for the professional clergy, the freshness, vitality, and radical influence of the church began to dramatically wane. But, many will counter, what real difference does it make who does the mentoring?

I became a Christ-follower at age 17. I was extremely blessed that my first church experience was one that profoundly impacted my view on ministry in the best possible way. The pastor of the church, Dave Anderson, was a tremendous expositor of the word, loved evangelism, and was totally committed to discipleship. He is the one who first mentored me and laid the spiritual foundation that I continue to build on to this day.

But as influential as Dave was in my life, equally influential were some other deeply committed men in the church who stayed in the working world. One was a pharmacist, who knew the word of God deeply and had a tremendous gift for exhortation which blessed all of us. Another was an engineer. On weekdays his commute to Houston was an hour each way. He used the time to memorize scripture and also was consistently discipling other men. Another was a successful hardware salesman who taught a weekly bible study on Friday nights in his home to well over a hundred high school and college students. Each of these men were deep in the word (none had gone to seminary or bible college), fully sold out to Christ, discipling others, and doing a great job in the working world. In reality they were all disciples of Christ first and foremost, and their occupation was simply their disguise for slipping into enemy territory to carry out their God-given assignment.

At the time I had no idea how deeply God was using these men to impact me. As a direct result of what I saw modeled, when I took my first job after college as a teaching tennis pro, their influence lingered with me. Like each of these men, I saw myself first and foremost as a disciple of Christ disguised as a tennis pro. My primary purpose on the courts was in some form or fashion to reflect the surprising life of Christ. My most important task in Midland was to win and disciple others. Only secondarily was it to make money helping people improve their game. Little did I realize at the time how rare my formative church experience was in the Christian world in America. Yet this was absolutely normative, run-of-the-mill Christianity in the early church.

What I saw modeled was a huge part of the magic of the early church. Regular, everyday people in the working world were being used by God to pass His life-changing word on to those in their own natural sphere of influence.

We have seen that Paul's (and our) first weapon of attack was the word of God. But accompanying the word of God was a vital second weapon of attack. It was the fire of God in his soul as he communicated the truths of scripture.

Second weapon of attack—the fire of God. *"...But also in power, and in the Holy Spirit and in much assurance,"* (I Thess. 1:5.) Call it what you will—passion, conviction, zeal, enthusiasm, unction— it is the fire of God in the soul of man. Jeremiah knew it. *"Then I said, 'I will not make mention of Him, nor speak anymore in His name.' But His word was in my heart like a burning fire shut up in my bones; I was weary of holding it back, And I could not,"* (Jer. 20:9.)

Jesus knew it. *"...Zeal for Your house has eaten Me up,"* (Jn. 2:17.)

Amy Carmichael knew it. "*Make me Thy fuel, O Flame of God.*"

John Wesley knew it. He was once asked the secret to his preaching. His response? "*I set myself on fire and people come to watch me burn.*"

I'm simply going to call this second weapon of attack "holy passion." I recognize that not all passion is godly or holy by a long shot. And that even within Christendom, not all passion is genuinely God-wrought passion. But for all the misuses and abuses of this thing called passion, it still remains a vital commodity for radical Christianity. Why?

There are several reasons I believe, but one in particular stands out as especially important. **Passion heightens credibility.** Let me say it again, passion engenders new levels of credibility! A.T. Robertson writes, *"It is not a preacher's wisdom but conviction which imparts itself to others. Nothing gives life but life. Real flame alone kindles another flame."*

The flip side is that lack of passion in things of vital importance tends to hamstring credibility. When Ghandi was investigating Christianity as a law student in South Africa, he tried several different churches. He would sometimes fall asleep during the sermon and would chide himself when he awoke for dozing off. At first he felt very guilty for doing so. That was until he began looking around and seeing that many of the church members were sleeping themselves! That was one of the several things that caused him to dismiss Christianity.

I think it can be easily argued that Nazi Germany could never have occurred apart from passion. If Hitler had given his speeches like most math lectures, there is no way the people would have followed him. Now obviously his was an awful passion, a demonic passion—but clearly a very persuasive passion. And that brings us to a very important point concerning effective and powerful communication. **How something is communicated is vital to the believability of what is communicated.** The light in the eyes, the vibrancy in the voice, and the eagerness about the message are all telltale signs of whether we *really* believe what we are talking about. As J. Oswald Sanders put it, *"People love to follow a person who believes his beliefs."*

There is a wonderful story concerning diamond magnate Harry Winston in regards to this. Winston assigned a salesman to show a prospective buyer one of his finest diamonds. When the salesman presented the diamond to the man, he described the expensive stone by pointing out all its fine technical features. The individual listened and praised the stone but turned away and said, "It's a wonderful stone but not exactly what I wanted."

Winston, who had been watching the presentation from a distance, stopped the man and asked, "Do you mind if I show you the diamond once again?" He agreed and Winston presented the same stone. But, instead of talking about the technical features of the stone, Winston spoke spontaneously about his own genuine admiration of the diamond and what a rare thing of beauty it was. Abruptly, the customer changed his mind and bought the diamond. While he was waiting for the diamond to be packaged and brought to him, the man turned to Winston and asked, "Why did I buy it from you when I had no difficulty saying no to your salesman?"

Winston replied, "The salesman is one of the best in the business and he knows more about diamonds than I do. I pay him a good salary for what he knows. But I would gladly pay him twice as much, if I could put into him something I have and he lacks. You see, he knows diamonds, but I love them."

Paul, Silas, and Timothy *knew* the gospel. They knew it very well for that matter. But just as importantly, they *loved* it. You could tell by the way they described it. You could feel the unconscious excitement rising up within them as they began pointing people to Christ. You couldn't miss the new light that went on in their eyes when they described God's astonishing offer of salvation through His Son's death. The intensity that gripped them when they spoke of Jesus was palpable. And it was real. Oh, so very real. The fire of God had come. And this God-birthed fire was critical for their message to be made credible and compelling to those watching and listening. Even if the listeners didn't buy into what the messenger was saying there was no way to discount the sincerity and blood earnestness of the messengers themselves. So let me say it again: passion heightens credibility!

There is a fascinating example of this in the life of great English evangelist George Whitefield. Whitefield was an amazingly gifted orator, but most of all loved His Lord and the gospel he preached. Often tears would run down his cheeks as he sought to point out the unfathomable love of God for men.

David Hume, the well-known Scottish philosopher and historian in the 18th Century, was also a Deist. He didn't believe in virtually anything concerning the bible and Christ, but still thought it worthwhile to travel 20 miles to hear Whitefield preach. About five o'clock one morning, he was going down the street in London. He came around the corner and went straight into the hands of another man who said:

"Why aren't you David Hume?"

"Yes."

"Where are you going at this early hour?"

"I'm going to hear George Whitefield preach," replied Hume.

"You don't believe a word Whitefield preaches," said the man.

"No," Hume answered, "but he does!"

Exactly! The servant of God who is owned by a Spirit-wrought passion that is unquestionably sincere is one of the most compelling sights around. Even to unbelievers.

It's important to note at this point that passion exhibits itself differently through different personalities. George Whitefield and Jonathan Edwards would be great illustrations of this. These two men of God were contemporaries and held immense respect for one another. They both knew the fire of God personally, and it was inescapably noticeable in their teaching and preaching. But in very different ways.

Whitefield was exuberant, often waving his arms, raising and lowering the tone of his voice, frequently weeping. Sarah Edwards, the wife of Jonathan Edwards, wrote to her brother of him, *"He is a born orator. You have already heard of his deep-toned, yet clear and melodious voice. O it is perfect music to listen to that alone! . . . You remember that David Hume thought it worth going 20 miles to hear him speak; and Garrick [*an actor who envied Whitefield's gifts*] said, 'He could move men to tears . . . in pronouncing the word Mesopotamia.' . . . It is truly wonderful to see what a spell this preacher often casts over an audience by proclaiming the simplest truths of the Bible."*

Cornelius Winter, Whitefield's associate wrote, *"I hardly ever knew him go through a sermon without weeping . . . sometimes he exceedingly wept, stamped loudly and passionately, and was frequently so overcome, that, for a few seconds, you would suspect he never could recover; and when he did, nature required some little time to compose himself."*

Jonathan Edwards on the other hand was far more reserved, very precise in his wording, and when he preached he normally read from his manuscript which he held near to his face because of weak eyes. But his passion was still very, very real. Only in a different way.

Samuel Hopkins, one of Edwards's students wrote, *"He had not a strong, loud voice, but appeared with such gravity and solemnity... His words often discovered a great degree of inward fervor, without much noise or external emotion, and fell with great weight on the minds of his hearers. He made but little motion of his head or hands in the desk, but spake as to discover the motion of his own heart, which tended in the most natural and effectual manner to move and affect others."*

Though Edwards's passion was not as visibly demonstrative as Whitefield's; it was no less real. When we speak of the importance of passion, it is important to recognize that the fire of God can express itself in very different ways according to the log it is engulfing. But it *will be* seen and felt, whatever the servant of God's personality and gifting.

Finally, it is vital to distinguish passion for a *cause* from passion for a *Person*. Paul's great passion in life was not evangelism, church planting, or ministry. It was a Person. The Person. Nowhere does he better describe this white hot passion better than the third chapter of Philippians. *"But what things were gain to me, these I have counted loss for Christ. Yet indeed I also count all things loss for the excellence of the knowledge of Christ Jesus my Lord, for whom I have suffered the loss of all things, and count them as rubbish, that I may gain Christ and be found in Him, not having my own righteousness, which is from the law, but that which is through faith in Christ, the righteousness which is from God by faith; that I may know Him and the power of His resurrection, and the fellowship of His sufferings, being conformed to His death, if, by any means, I may attain to the resurrection from the dead," (* Phil. 3:7-11.)

As zealous as Paul was for seeing Christ proclaimed, churches established, believers being built up, etc., he never lost his primary passion in life—an ever deepening, soul-ravishing love affair with the One Who blocked his path, forgave his sins, implanted His Spirit, and completely rerouted his life. It was his passion for a Person that carried him through good days and bad, and enabled him to say at the twilight of his life, *"For this reason I also suffer these things; nevertheless I am not ashamed, for I know Whom I have believed and am persuaded that He is able to keep what I have committed to Him until that Day," (* II Tim. 1:12.) Notice he didn't say, "for I know *what* I have believed," but "*Whom* I have believed." When the chips are down it is ultimately a Who rather than a what that carries us through. And it was his passion for a Person rather than a cause that not only sustained him over the long haul, but brought compelling authenticity to his glad proclamation of the God's word.

Dangerous Christians are more passionate about the Person of Christ than their work for Christ. This is a subtle distinction but a vital one. Ministry can become an idol just like anything else. This is *exactly* what had happened to the believers in Ephesus:

"I know your deeds and your toil and perseverance, and that you cannot tolerate evil men, and you put to the test those who call themselves apostles, and they are not, and you found them to be false; and you have perseverance and have endured for My name's sake, and have not grown weary. But I have this against you, that you have left your first love. Therefore remember from where you have fallen, and repent and do the deeds you did at first; or else I am coming to you and will remove your lampstand out of its place—unless you repent," (Rev. 2:2-5.)

Christ begins by genuinely commending them for their ministry and service. And their work for the Lord was impressive indeed. But then He goes on to rebuke them for their idolatry. But what, you ask, was their idol? Ministry itself. "*But I have this against you, that you have left your first love. Therefore remember from where you have fallen, and repent and do the deeds you did at first.*" They had fallen from the heights of loving foremost the Person of Christ, had unwittingly left their first love, and replaced it with service for Christ. And good as ministry is, it is still an idol if it comes before our love affair with Christ. They had slowly over time exchanged their passion for a Person for passion for a cause.

I have seen this a thousand times over in the church today. I have seen this a thousand times over in my own life. It is so easy to let time alone with the King quietly slip away in exchange for the pursuit of making our lives count for the Kingdom. But one thing I am absolutely convinced of by scripture, history, and personal experience—every servant of God must make a radical choice if he or she is going to be a game changer. A choice of monumental proportions and remarkable consequences. Simply put, it is this: **knowing God is more important than serving God.** Pure and simple. Not as important. More important. And that's where we sometimes balk at what that will mean personally and practically.

As we grow in Christ, opportunities for service usually multiply. Before long, we are forced to make choices between which opportunities to take. And this is where the danger begins to lurk. We become more concerned about the choice *between* ministry needs than the choice *over* ministry needs. And I can tell you from my own experience and the testimonies of many others, when spending time at the feet of Jesus takes backseat to serving Him, we are well on our way to Martha's dilemma, *"worried and troubled about many things," (*Lk.10:41.)

Henry Martyn was greatly used by the Lord as a missionary and bible translator in the early 1800s. He wrote of the secret of his fruitfulness, *"My principal enjoyment is the enjoyment of His presence."* But he also wrote of the danger of putting ministry for Christ ahead of intimacy with Christ. *"The want of private devotional reading and shortness of prayers through incessant sermon making has produced much strangeness between God and my soul."* I for one am deeply encouraged by his honest admission. Maybe there's hope for all of us if someone of the stature of Henry Martyn struggled with choosing intimacy over ministry.

This choice was well exemplified by another of God's great game changers—George Mueller. This Englishman was an incredibly fruitful servant of God. During his lifetime he helped build five large orphanages housing some ten thousand orphans, of whom approximately one-third came to know Christ. He received and gave away some seven and a half million dollars to support hundreds of missionaries. He was heavily involved in Christian publishing and the founding of many educational and religious institutions. From age seventy to eighty-four he traveled more than two hundred thousand miles in forty-two different countries, preaching the gospel to more than three million people.

His secret? Believing that his most important calling was spending time at Christ's feet, just like Mary, (Lk. 10:38-42.) In his journal he writes:

"While I was staying at Nailsworth, it pleased the Lord to teach me a truth...the benefit of which I have not lost, though now, while preparing the eighth edition for the press, more than forty years have passed away. The point is this: I saw more clearly than ever, that the first great and primary business to which I ought attend every day was, to have my soul happy in the Lord. The first thing to be concerned about was not, how much I might serve the Lord, how I might glorify the Lord; but how I might get my soul in a happy state, and how my inner man may be nourished."

I love the way he puts it: *the first great and primary business to which I ought attend every day was, to have my soul happy in the Lord.* The fragrant, fruitful life of George Muller is a powerful and lasting testimony to the all-surpassing importance of giving preeminent attention to our roots. Not just rote bible study or mechanical praying, but deep, passionate, white-hot, God-seeking. Dangerous Christians choose this first and foremost as their major; everything else becomes a minor, important as they may be.

Inextricably linked to holy passion is dependence upon the Holy Spirit. You cannot get one without the other. Paul clearly recognized that communicating the word of God without desperate dependence upon the Spirit of God would lead to what is popularly known as "dead orthodoxy." Christ could not have made it clearer. *"...and those who worship Him must worship in spirit and truth,"* (Jn. 4:24.) Truth is not enough and Spirit is not enough. But truth communicated in the supernatural power of the Holy Spirit is a force that even hell cannot reckon with. And that was the unique power of the early church. *"Therefore, brethren, seek out from among you seven men of good reputation, full of the Holy Spirit and wisdom, whom we may appoint over this business,"* (Acts 6:3.) *"And they were not able to resist the wisdom and the spirit by which he spoke,"* (Acts 6:10.)

That was also one of the very strong features of the Moravian church. Zinzendorf stressed again and again that the work was God's from beginning to end—people were only His tools. Dr. Ryoo notes, *"The Moravians carried out their mission through the power of the Holy Spirit. They believed that missionary activity is a part of the divine plan of God as He uses committed people of God through the Holy Spirit. In delivering the message of Jesus Christ, the Moravians depended on the presence and work of the Holy Spirit. They believed that it is the Holy Spirit Who searches the souls for His lost people and opens their hearts to respond to the preaching of the missionary. In this sense, 'the Holy Spirit is the only missionary, and human beings are agents of the Spirit.'"* Zinzendorf used to tell his departing missionaries, *"You are not going anywhere the Holy Spirit has not already gone."* Dangerous Christians' highest goal in ministry is simply to "*keep in step with the Spirit,*" (Gal. 5:25) and make themselves open conduits through which the word of God and the Spirit of God can flow unhindered.

Third weapon of attack—the glory of God. *"...As you know what kind of men we were among you for your sake."* We have now the final weapon of attack in their arsenal. They not only brought the word of God accompanied by the fire of God.

But they also brought the third critical commodity of the glory of God. In other words they put the surprising-ness of God on public display.

You see, the surprising-ness of God and the glory of God are one in the same. Everything about God is stunning, breath-taking, astonishing...in other words—surprising. So when we are called to glorify God it is something far more than simply living morally upright, squeaky clean, doctrinally pure lifestyles. It is living in such a way that people are caught off guard with unexpected displays of radical, Christ-empowered godliness. So what did these displays look like among the Thessalonians? In other words, what did Paul have in mind when he said, "*... What kind of men we were among you...?*" Fortunately the answer is given to us very specifically in I Thess. 2:1-12. Here is a sampling of some of the things that caught the Thessalonians off guard and opened them up to receiving the gospel from Paul and his companions.

Surprising Resilience: *"But even after we had suffered before and were spitefully treated at Philippi, as you know, we were bold in our God to speak to you the gospel of God in much conflict,"* (I Thess. 2:2.)

One of the primary factors which caused the unbelievers of the first three centuries to take note of this new cult called Christianity was how these early saints responded to persecution and unfair suffering. Many of them went to their deaths singing praises to Christ and praying for their persecutors. Others had homes confiscated, jobs taken away, were beaten, and were separated from their families. As the writer of Hebrews put it, "*You* *joyfully accepted the plundering of your goods," (*Heb. 10:34.) Few things more powerfully accentuate the credibility of the gospel than a God-honoring response to undeserved suffering. Paul, Silas, and Timothy weathered the storms of physical persecution and undeserved suffering in Philippi and Thessalonica with surprising resilience. They neither grew bitter nor timid, and they continued moving forward in God's strength with God's gospel.

Adoniram Judson went to Burma in 1813 to spread the gospel in this very difficult country. At one stage earlier in his life he was caught up in the Anglo-Burmese war. During a seventeen month stint in Ava Prison, his mistreatment was horrific and he picked up some ugly scars made by the chains and iron shackles that cruelly bound him. When released, he sought permission to take the gospel to yet another province, but the antagonistic ruler indignantly denied his request, saying: *"My people are not fools enough to listen to anything a missionary might say, but I fear they might be impressed by your scars and turn to your religion!"* Judson's sufferings not only resulted in scars, they also resulted in heightening the credibility and authenticity of his message. His scars became God's platform.

Dangerous Christians may very well not experience actual physical persecution or scars. But mark it well, they most assuredly will suffer. Ministry that matters does not come cheaply. It is normally purchased through shed tears, dashed hopes, and an aching heart. Paul writes, *"Blessed be the God and Father of our Lord Jesus Christ, the Father of mercies and God of all comfort, Who comforts us in all our tribulation, that we may be able to comfort those who are in any trouble, with the comfort with which we ourselves are comforted by God,"* (II Cor. 1:3, 4.) I'm struck by the phrase *that we may be able to comfort…with the comfort with which we ourselves are comforted by God.* The word used for "comfort" is just as easily translated "encourage." In other words, the most powerful encouragers in the body of Christ are wounded encouragers, broken encouragers, bleeding encouragers. Encouragers who give away not themselves, but "the comfort" God poured into them while they were being pounded on His anvil. Oswald Chambers puts it so well:

"If you are going to be used by God, He will take you through a multitude of experiences that are not meant for you at all, they are meant to make you useful in His hands, and to enable you to understand what transpires in other souls so that you will never be surprised at what you come across."

God never wastes any blows in our life. Each one is carefully scrutinized and sovereignly orchestrated by the One Who "*…does not afflict willingly (lit. "from His heart") nor grieve the children of men,*" (Lam. 3:33.) Though He does not afflict willingly, He does afflict certainly. And sometimes, brutally. And knowing whether this trial is His causative will or His permissive will does not keep the tears from rolling down one's cheek. But, as Chambers puts it, these brutal afflictions "*…enable you to understand what transpires in other souls.*"

Being used by God requires more than an understanding of the scriptures (though this is vital); it also requires an understanding of the soul. Nothing, but nothing, equips us for that quite like the classroom of suffering. The woman who has lost her husband can speak to another grieving woman who has lost her husband with a power that those outside this heartache simply cannot. Parents of a disabled child know the reservoir of pain which other parents of a disabled child continually carry around, and therefore can encourage more deeply than those who have never faced this trial. A couple who has experienced the devastation of multiple miscarriages will be helped most by another couple who has walked the same heart-wrenching path. Charles Spurgeon, who suffered much during his life, wrote:

"There is no learning sympathy except by suffering. It cannot be studied in a book, it must be written on the heart. You must go through the fire if you would have sympathy with others who tread the glowing coals. You must yourself bear the cross if you would feel for those whose life is a burden to them."

We are only on the anvil for a short time until we are permanently and joyously removed from its grip. In the meantime, every blow is a bond uniquely connecting us with others who have felt the same pain. Each heartache, each tragedy, each difficulty serves as a bridge over which the supernatural encouragement of God to us can make its way into others' lives. Each blow is also a platform. Like Paul and his companions, our surprising response to suffering sets the stage for others to take our Christianity far more seriously than if our lives had been rain free. Jonathan Edwards put it so well, *"True virtue never appears so lovely as when it is most oppressed; and the divine excellency of real Christianity is never exhibited with such advantage as when under the greatest trials."*

Surprising Sincerity: *"For our exhortation did not come from error or uncleanness, nor was it in deceit. But as we have been* *approved by God to be entrusted with the gospel, even so we speak, not as pleasing men, but God who tests our hearts. For neither at any time did we use flattering words, as you know, nor a cloak for covetousness—God is witness. Nor did we seek glory from men, either from you or from others,"* (I Thess. 2:3-6.)

In a world rife with deceit, hypocrisy, and religious charlatanism, the unmistakable sincerity and authenticity of these men stood out in blazing contrast. Their message was the uncompromised, undiluted, whole counsel of God's word. Their motivation was laser focused on pleasing their audience of One, regardless of how their hearers responded. Unlike the vast majority of roaming orators and teachers of the day, they radically stiff-armed the two primary motivations which controlled those speakers—greed (*"nor a cloak of covetousness")* and fame ("*nor did we seek glory from men.*") Clearly nothing has changed in 2,000 years.

One of the most critically important characteristics of a dangerous Christian is unquestionable sincerity and penetrating authenticity. People instinctively know when it's there and equally, when it is not. Cliff Barrows recounts, "*In 1945, I was with him (Billy Graham) in London, and he had a visit with Winston Churchill and some of the members of his Cabinet…As he left, Winston Churchill turned to his Cabinet members and said, 'There goes a sincere young man.'"* There can be no doubt that Graham's sincerity and authenticity has been a central pillar in his worldwide ministry.

Surprising Purity: "*You are witnesses, and God also, how devoutly and justly and blamelessly we behaved ourselves among you who believe,"* (I Thess. 2:10.)

In a world far more sex-crazed than even our own, one in which the shameless indulgence of physical appetites was seen as normative and necessary; Paul, Silas, and Timothy broke the mold. One of the strongest features of Christianity in the early church was its unwavering belief in the absolute sacredness of marriage and the marriage bed. As the writer of Hebrews states, "*Marriage is honorable among all, and the bed undefiled; but fornicators and adulterers God will judge.*" Women in particular were drawn to this unheard of reality.

Surprising Toil: *"For you remember, brethren, our labor and toil; for laboring night and day, that we might not be a burden to any of you, we preached to you the gospel of God,"* (I Thess. 2:9.)

One of the truly fascinating elements of their surprise factor was the way they leveraged their everyday jobs for Kingdom purposes. While they had the right to be at least partially supported by these new Thessalonian believers, they chose to bypass it. "… *when we might have made demands as apostles of Christ,"* (I Thess. 2:6.) I think there were at least two excellent and instructive reasons for this.

The first was the *credibility* factor. As long as they were fully supporting themselves through their job (tent making), no one could possibly suspect or say that they were ministering for the money. This was and is no small issue. I refer again to the words of Michael Green concerning the first century believers, "*They went everywhere gossiping the gospel; they did it naturally, enthusiastically, and with the conviction of those who are not paid to say that sort of thing. Consequently, they were taken seriously and the movement spread...*" I'm so struck by his last statement, "*with the conviction of those who are not paid to say that sort of thing. Consequently, they were taken seriously.*" I can tell you that after being a pastor for more than 30 years, when people discover you're clergy, walls immediately go up. Not always, but much of the time. Suddenly the credibility and relatability you had with this person is lost or at least greatly jeopardized. Not that it's intentional or mean spirited in any way. It's just that when they discover you're a professional, your God-talk ceases to carry the weight it did when they still perceived you as one of them. This is why the clergy/laity distinction, which was utterly absent in the early years of the church, has become one of its most devastating heresies. Not only theologically, but also very, very practically.

The second was the *opportunity* factor. **Paul, Silas, and Timothy did not see working as tentmakers to be a distraction from ministry.** They saw it as it truly is—an opportunity for ministry. An opportunity to naturally and easily share the gospel with fellow workers and customers. An opportunity to flesh out one's faith in the midst of the challenges and pressures of the working world. An opportunity to demonstrate that Christianity is not a Sunday-only affair, but an everyday adventure and calling. It was through tent making that Paul led Priscilla and Aquila to the Lord and that the Corinthian church was birthed. "*And he found a certain Jew named Aquila, born in Pontus, who had recently come from Italy with his wife Priscilla (because Claudius had commanded all the Jews to depart from Rome); and he came to* *them. So, because he was of the same trade, he stayed with them and worked; for by occupation they were tentmakers. And he reasoned in the synagogue every Sabbath, and persuaded both Jews and Greeks,"* (Acts 18:2-4.)

With the arrival of the clergy/laity distinction, the workplace tragically began to lose its dignity and viability as being one of the most central and crucial locations for gospel circulation. Ironically, Communism spread largely through the work place being harnessed and utilized as one of the premier opportunities for the advance of Socialism. One of the favorite sayings of the Communist party was, *"Every Communist a leader, every factory a fortress."* One former Communist worker described his life as a Communist:

"You got up in the morning and as you shaved you were thinking of the jobs you would do for Communism that day. You went down to breakfast and read **The Daily Worker** *to get the Party line—to get the shot and shell for a fight in which you were already involved. You read every item in the paper wondering how you might be able to use it for the cause. On the bus or the train, on my way to work, I read* **The Daily Worker** *as ostentatiously as I could, holding it up so that others might read the headlines and perhaps be influenced by them. I took two copies of the paper with me; the second one I left in the seat in the hope that someone would pick it up and read it.*

When I got to work, I kept **The Daily Worker** *circulating... At lunch... I made a practice of sitting with different groups in order to spread my influence as widely as I could. I did not thrust Communism down their throats but steered our conversations in such a* *way that they could be brought round to politics…or the campaigns which the Party was conducting at the time.*"

The church was most dangerous to the kingdom of darkness during the days that the workplace was best utilized as one of the most central avenues for fleshing out and verbalizing the gospel.

The Moravians understood this well. The vast, vast majority of Moravians had full time jobs, including their missionaries. But they viewed their occupations as especially fertile ground for being able to share the gospel naturally and credibly with those they came in contact with. *"Zinzendorf felt that not only would their practice and teaching of trades lift the economic level of the people to whom they were sent, but the exercising of the trades would also provide a way of natural interaction with these same people,"* writes Dr. Kenneth Mulholland. Notice the two main reasons Zinzendorf gave for why he wanted his people to remain fully engaged in the working world. First, they powerfully blessed the people around them. They helped elevate these people's standard of living by the wise business practices they modeled and even taught. Secondly, it provided "*natural interaction*" with the people they were seeking to reach. Both of these are critical.

A friend of mine named Jim went on staff with a major Christian organization to be a missionary in Colombia. Apparently he didn't get the memo that as a missionary he wasn't supposed to have a secular job of any kind. Jim is an entrepreneur at heart and so one of the first things he did was open a barbeque restaurant in the city. He hired only national workers, trained them, and provided them with excellent salaries and benefits. Before long the business took off big time. People loved him for his great food, caring personality, and especially the way he cared for his staff. As a result he led many, many Colombians to the Lord and had more people to disciple than he could handle.

Then one day the mission organization back in the US got wind of what he was doing. On his next furlough they grilled him on why he was wasting valuable time with a secular job. He tried to explain his reasons but didn't get very far. But finally they discovered something that enabled him to keep the restaurant open. He had monumentally more new converts and disciples than any of the other missionaries who were only doing bible teaching!

Something we have done in our church is to require that every staff member have at least a part-time job in the working world. Including me, the senior pastor. So far we've only seen benefits from this with no downside. First, it keeps us fresh and current on the unbelieving world. It's been a great reminder that the vast majority of the world doesn't care if the rapture is pre, mid, or post. That only a miniscule percentage of people know whether they are pre-millennial, post-millennial, or a-millennial. And even less care. Mainly they're just worrying about an adequate paycheck, raising their kids, and whether the extra-marital affair is worth it or not. Second, it provides such a natural platform to talk about the Lord without having to use the clergy card. Interestingly, we are finding that more and more of our visitors and even joining members are coming from the contacts we make in our job venues.

Now, please hear me well. I am **not** saying that all pastors and Christian workers should get part-time jobs. Clearly there is no verse in the scriptures commanding this. Every situation is different and the key is to be sensitive to God's calling, wherever we are and however he would have us spend our time.

Surprising Love: *But we were gentle among you, just as a nursing mother cherishes her own children. So, affectionately longing for you, we were well pleased to impart to you not only the gospel of God, but also our own lives, because you had become dear to us....as you know how we exhorted, and comforted, and charged every one of you, as a father does his own children, that you would walk worthy of God who calls you into His own kingdom and glory,"* (I Thess. 2:7, 8, 11, 12.)

Paul, Silas, and Timothy understood and practiced one of the most important aspects of being a game changer. **Before you can change a life, you must win a heart.** Floyd McClung put it well, "*People don't know how much you know until they know how much you care.*" And this they did in spades with the Thessalonians. The quality of love described here is remarkable in that it is so well balanced. It was characterized first by the warmth, tenderness, and heart-felt compassion which is exhibited most clearly in "*a nursing mother.*" Secondly, it was balanced with the strong love of a deeply caring father who "*exhorted, and comforted, and charged"* his beloved children that they "*would walk worthy of God.*" What is remarkable is that so very often love which is strong in providing warmth and acceptance is often weak in providing direction. And love that is strong in providing direction is all too often weak in providing warmth and acceptance. Joshua Swartz writes along these lines, "*Truth without charity is often intolerant and even persecuting, as charity* *without truth is weak in concession and untrustworthy in judgment. But charity, loyal to the truth and rejoicing in it, has the wisdom of the serpent with the harmlessness of the dove."* But Paul and his companions became earthly conduits through which the strong, warm love of God was able to make its way into the hearts and lives of the Thessalonians. And having won their hearts, they were used by God to change their lives. Forever.

The word of God...the fire of God...the glory of God. Or to put it another way, the word of God, holy passion, surprising lives. These were the big three. We will see in the next chapter that these are the exact three things which went on to characterize the Thessalonians' lives and ministry. And to this day these still are the big three. They provide the full spectrum of true spirituality, for they provide divine fodder for the mind (word of God), divine heat for the heart (holy passion), and divine credibility for the life (surprising lives). It is through these three that the head, the heart, and the hand come together in perfect union and full-orbed spirituality.

Gate crashers and game changers are fanatical about these three. Of course, it is simply another way of saying, "Let Christ live His life through us." And if He is even remotely allowed to live His life through us, we will find His word flowing through us both spontaneously and intentionally. We will be aflame with a holy passion which is directed far more toward a Person than a cause. And we will blow wide open the stereotype so many people have of predictable, joyless, condescending Christianity. In a word, we will look more and more like Jesus. The real Jesus, that is.

Chapter 6

THE MAKING OF A DANGEROUS CHRISTIAN

A disciple is one who has a mind aflame with the truth of God, a heart ablaze with the love of God, and a will fired with a passion for the glory of God.
—J. Oswald Sanders

CRAWL, WALK, RUN. THERE'S NO way around it. Nobody gets fast forwarded to running. Every baby begins his or her pilgrimage on this planet by learning first to crawl. Then the time comes when they graduate to walking. And finally the day comes when they discover the delights of running. Nobody, but nobody, gets air lifted from crawling to running; everyone is subject to nature's law of developing mobility.

What is true in the natural realm is exactly the same in the spiritual realm. Dangerous Christians don't become dangerous in a day. There is a threefold process which takes them from spiritually crawling...to walking...to running. And this process is clearly delineated for us in the opening chapter of I Thessalonians.

"And you became followers of us and of the Lord, having received the word in much affliction, with joy of the Holy Spirit, so that you became examples to all in Macedonia and Achaia who believe. For from you the word of the Lord has sounded forth, not only in Macedonia and Achaia, but also in every place. Your faith toward

God has gone out, so that we do not need to say anything," (I Thess. 1:6-8.)

The Crawl Stage: *"And you became followers of us…"*

In the beginning stages of our walk with God we are very much dependent upon other, more mature believers to guide and mentor us. We look to them to help us understand the bible, what Christian books to read, how to pray, etc. Unconsciously, it becomes very natural for us to imitate them and their approach to spirituality. In fact the Greek word used here for "followers" is the very word we get "mimic" from. This is why many translations render it "*and you became imitators of us…*" Eugene Peterson puts it like this in The Message. *"You paid careful attention to the way we lived among you, and determined to live that way yourselves."*

Just as a young child naturally mimics so much of his parent's behavior and attitudes, new believers tend to do the exact same thing with their spiritual mentors and leaders. There is nothing wrong with this; it is simply a natural and normal part of our spiritual development. It is part and parcel of being "*babes in Christ*," (I Cor. 3:1.)

The Walk Stage: "*…and of the Lord…*"

This is the crucial next progression in spiritual maturity. **The walk stage is when there is a significant shift of dependency.** It is the moving away from relying primarily upon other human beings to now relying primarily on the Lord Himself. It is when a believer begins tasting the unrivaled joy of hearing from God directly, of experiencing Him first-hand in ways they had not previously. J. Oswald Sanders has such a great word on this:

"Christ is claiming the ability to satisfy the deepest need of the human heart, yet we are strangely reluctant to come directly to Him. We will attend ceremonies and observe sacraments. We will follow men and congregate in meetings. We will frequent camps and conventions. We will listen to priests and preachers—anything, it would seem, except come personally and alone into the presence of Christ. But He is absolutely intolerant. He will quench our spiritual thirst personally and not by proxy."

The walk stage is when we begin to *"come personally and alone into the presence of Christ."* It is when we refuse to be spiritually nourished "*by proxy,*" i.e. other humans, and we determine to personally sink our roots deeply and fiercely into the true and living God. There is an outstanding example of the difference between the crawl and walk stages in the life of Samuel as described in I Sam. 3.

Our first description of Samuel shows clearly that he is in the crawl stage. "*Now the boy Samuel ministered to the Lord before Eli…*" Note the phrase, "*before Eli," (*I Sam. 3:1.) Eli was his spiritual mentor and guide. The next thing we read about is God's first hand calling of the young boy Samuel. *"…while Samuel was lying down…the Lord called Samuel. And he answered, 'Here I am!' So he ran to Eli and said, 'Here I am, for you called me,*" (I Sam. 3:3-5.) When God calls, Samuel runs to Eli for he does not yet recognize God's voice for himself. Eli tells him to go lie down for he had not called Samuel. The exact same thing happens another time. This time we are given the root issue in a parenthetical statement: *(Now Samuel did not yet know the Lord, nor was the word of the Lord yet revealed to him.)* Clearly Samuel knew *about* the Lord, but did not yet know Him intimately, first-hand. Samuel was still in the crawl stage.

A third time God calls and for a third time Samuel goes to Eli. Then we read, *"Then Eli perceived that the Lord had called the boy. Therefore Eli said to Samuel, "Go, lie down; and it shall be, if He calls you, that you must say, 'Speak, Lord, for Your servant hears.'" So Samuel went and lay down in his place,"* (I Sam. 3:8, 9.)

And now we read of the beginning of Samuel's walking stage. *"Now the Lord came and stood and called as at other times, 'Samuel! Samuel!' And Samuel answered, 'Speak, for Your servant hears.'"* And for the first time Samuel hears the word of God for himself, apart from any human intervention. He also delivers the message to Eli which he had heard from God alone, (I Sam. 3:11-18.)

And then we read the powerful difference that experiencing and hearing from God personally makes: *"So Samuel grew, and the Lord was with him and let none of his words fall to the ground. And all Israel from Dan to Beersheba knew that Samuel had been established as a prophet of the Lord. Then the Lord appeared again in Shiloh. For the Lord revealed Himself to Samuel in Shiloh by the word of the Lord,"* (I Sam. 3:19-21.) I'm particularly struck by the phrase *and let none of his words fall to the ground.*

Ah, the power of hearing from God first-hand! The influence of a man or woman who pays the price to personally know God deeply! John Wesley wrote in his diary, *"Here then I am, far from the busy ways of men. I sit down alone; only God is here. In his presence I open, I read his Book…and what I learn, I teach."* I love his phrase *only God is here.*

The Thessalonians had moved from crawling to walking. They had become first century Samuels, wreaking havoc upon the kingdom of darkness. But what of today?

In a strange way, especially here in America, one of our greatest blessings has also become one of our greatest hindrances. What I mean is this. We live in a world where one can hear off-the-chart, phenomenal teaching and preaching 24 hours a day. Christian books, downloads, videos, etc. abound in astonishing numbers and are so, so easily accessible. And we are all too often becoming Samuels at the beginning of the story without moving on to become Samuels at the end of the story.

We are living off what Christian leaders are saying about God and the Christian life. And that is precisely why we are not having more impact in our generation. Among pastors and Christian teachers I believe there is a substantial overdependence upon commentaries and others' sermons for understanding the passage and gaining speaking material. This is not to say that commentaries, sermons, etc., aren't extremely helpful; and certainly they can serve as important aids to any speaker's message. But aids they are, and aids they will ever be. They are the echoes of God's word but not the original shout. Commentaries can never take the place of first-hand wrestling with the word of God itself and experiencing the warmth, joy, and vitality of supernatural intersecting. Like the disciples on the Emmaus road, the heart cry of dangerous Christians is, *"Did not our heart burn within us while He talked with us on the road, and while He opened the Scriptures to us?"* (Lk.24:32.)

Game changers do not become dangerous by parroting what other spiritual leaders say about the word of God. They become dangerous by knowing God first hand, by frequently journeying into the land of solitude, and staying quiet long enough to hear His still, small voice. Howard Hendricks puts it so, so well:

"I am convinced that there are many Christians today to whom God is saying incisively, 'Go hide yourself.' That is a difficult assignment in a busy world. We are compulsive activists, and there are so many voices clamoring for our attention that it is easy to miss the voice of God in the process. You may be asking God to use you, to shape you, to mold you, to give you a cutting edge, not only in the present generation but, if the Lord tarries, in the next generation. ***But you will have nothing to say to this generation or the next unless God first speaks to you. The important thing is not what you read or what you hear in a school or in a conference from an individual who is simply an instrument in the hands of God. In the final analysis, the important thing is whether you hear from God Himself.*** *And if you do not hear from Him, then all that those men and women may tell you will not make sense, nor will it have its designed impact."*

To put it another way, the crawl stage is where other believers are the entrée and the Lord Himself is an appetizer. The walk stage is where the Lord Himself is the entrée and other believers are simply the appetizer.

The Run Stage: *"...having received the word in much affliction, with joy of the Holy Spirit, so that you became examples to all in Macedonia and Achaia who believe. For from you the word of the Lord has sounded forth, not only in Macedonia and Achaia, but* *also in every place. Your faith toward God has gone out, so that we do not need to say anything."*

Here is the final stage of the dangerous Christian. Crawling and walking are wonderful preparations for running, but it would be tragic to stop with only these two. Running is our final gear and a wonderful gift from our Creator. The Thessalonians were running full out and Paul was thrilled with their progress. What then did their spiritual running look like? It's very simple. They were now passing on to those in their natural sphere of influence the exact same things Paul, Silas, and Timothy had first brought to them. They had moved from being consumers to distributors and the results were that the gates of hell were being badly battered and others' lives were being mightily transformed. In the words of Isaiah, they had become, *"…trees of righteousness, the planting of the Lord, that He may be glorified,"* (Is. 61:3.)

What was it that Paul, Silas, and Timothy had brought to the Thessalonians? You'll remember from the last chapter that it was three things: the word of God, holy passion, and surprising lives. What things then were the Thessalonians trafficking in and passing along. Check this out. It was the very, very same things!

Word of God: *"For from you the word of the Lord has sounded forth…"*

The early saints lived and breathed the word of God. The scriptures were their fondest meditation and their foremost message. This was true not only of the Thessalonians but of the early believers who came after them. This is our earliest description of a worship service, passed along by Justin Martyr around 150 AD.

"And on the day called Sunday, all who live in cities or in the country gather together to one place, and the memoirs of the apostles or the writings of the prophets are read, as long as time permits; then, when the reader has ceased, the president verbally instructs, and exhorts to the imitation of these good things. Then we all rise together and pray, and, as we before said, when our prayer is ended, bread and wine and water are brought, and the president in like manner offers prayers and thanksgivings, according to his ability, and the people assent, saying Amen."

Note the amount of time in the service dedicated to the word of God. "*...and the memoirs of the apostles or the writings of the prophets are read, as long as time permits...*"

One of the very earliest letters we have comes from Polycarp, a disciple of the apostle John. As one scholar put it, the letter is "a mosaic of scriptures." In other words, the letter itself is saturated with the quoting of various scriptures. Here's just a short sample. I have left the quoted scriptures in italics:

"...and beareth fruit unto our Lord Jesus Christ, who endured to face even death for our sins, *whom God raised, having loosed the pangs of Hades; on whom, though ye saw Him not, ye believe with joy unutterable and full of glory*; unto which joy many desire to enter in; forasmuch as ye know that it is *by grace ye are saved, not of works*, but by the will of God through Jesus Christ. *Wherefore gird up your loins and serve God in fear* and truth, forsaking the vain and empty talking and the error of the many, *for that ye have believed on Him that raised our Lord Jesus Christ from the dead and gave unto him glory* and a throne on His right hand; unto whom all things were made subject that are in heaven and that are on the earth." Note how much of this letter is simply quoted, unedited scripture!

The Thessalonians followed in the footsteps of Paul and became first century megaphones for the eternal, unchanging, life-transforming word of God.

Please note that it doesn't say "from your elders the word of the Lord sounded forth." Or even, "from your leaders the word of the Lord sounded forth." No, a thousand times no! The word for "you" in the original is a plural "you," so it should be translated "for from all of you." Everyone was passing along the word of God spontaneously and intentionally. And this was one of the most central reasons the early church was so dangerous. Michael Green writes concerning the early church, *"The very fact that we are so imperfectly aware of how evangelism was carried out and by whom, should make us sensitive to the possibility that the little man, the unknown ordinary man, the man who left no literary remains was the prime agent in mission."* Elsewhere he states, *"Evangelism was the prerogative and duty of every church member. We have seen apostles and wandering prophets, nobles and paupers, intellectuals and fishermen all taking part enthusiastically in this primary task committed by Christ to his Church. The ordinary people of the Church saw it as their job: Christianity was supremely a lay movement, spread by informal missionaries...the spontaneous outreach of the total Christian community gave immense impetus to the movement from the very outset."*

Dangerous Christians are particularly dangerous because the primary message they offer the world and their "*casual contacts*" is the living, powerful, unchanging word of God.

Holy Passion: "*...the word of the Lord has sounded forth...*"

I think we find this holy passion in the word Paul uses for "*sounded forth*." He could have simply said "the word of the Lord went forth", or something equally tame. But he didn't. He chose a Greek word that was used to describe the peal of a lightning bolt or the sound of heavy thunder. It was also used to describe the sound of a loud trumpet calling men into battle. I don't believe it is a stretch at all to see holy passion undergirding how they passed along the word of God. This passion, this fire, this zeal was unquestionably part and parcel of the early church. Again Michael Green notes, "*with the Scriptures and prayer as their main weapons, backed up by their love, their burning zeal to share their faith with others, and the sheer quality of their living and dying that the early Christians set out to evangelize the world.*"

Milton L. Rudnick writes, "*...the early Christians were characterized by a compelling desire to offer others the incomparable blessing they had received through faith in Jesus Christ. What they had was simply too good to keep quiet about, too good to keep to themselves.*"

Dangerous Christians move strongly into their world with not only the word of God in their hands but also the fire of God in their bones. They bring this darkened world both light and heat. Just like John the Baptist, whom Jesus described as "*...a burning and shining lamp,*" (Jn. 6:35.) And most importantly, just like Jesus Himself.

Surprising Lives: "*...having received the word in much affliction, with joy of the Holy Spirit, so that you became examples to all* *in Macedonia and Achaia who believe... Your faith toward God has gone out, so that we do not need to say anything."*

Just as Paul, Silas, and Timothy had astonished the Thessalonians with unexpected displays of radical, Christ-empowered godliness, these same Thessalonians were now marching to the same drum beat. The word used here for "*examples*" was used to describe the mark or bruise that was left on the body after being physically assaulted. It also described the visible hoof print of a horse. In each case it described the unmistakable, tangible imprint of being impacted by a greater power or force. Which is exactly what the Thessalonians were doing. They had been deeply impacted not simply by a greater force but by a greater Person. And their lives bore the unmistakable scorch marks of heaven intersecting earth.

Like Paul, Silas, and Timothy; they were reflecting surprising resilience to the peoples *"not only in Macedonia and Achaia, but also in every place."* What made their resilience to undeserved suffering so surprising was that they *"received the word in much affliction, with joy of the Holy Spirit."* "*Much affliction*" coupled with "*joy of the Holy Spirit*" was a spectacle that shouted to the Thessalonians and those nearby that Jesus needs to be taken seriously. No god in their world could provide even a modicum of comfort or peace in the midst of such difficult times. Much less, joy.

Without a doubt, one of the most powerful arguments for Christianity in the early church was the astonishing way believers handled persecution and even death for the gospel's sake. In the second century Tertullian summed this up in his famous statement, *"The blood of martyrs is the seed of the Church."* Closely tied to this was the radically different way Christ followers viewed death. They demonstrated a palpable hope about which the pagan world knew nothing. In the catacombs of Rome we find many epitaphs of deceased men, women, and children. They are epitaphs of both Christians and pagans. The differences are remarkable. Among the pagan epitaphs we read:

"Live for the present hour, since we are sure of nothing else."

"I lift my hands against the gods who took me away at the age of twenty though I had done no harm."

"Once I was not. Now I am not. I know nothing about it, and it is no concern of mine."

"Traveler, curse me not as you pass, for I am in darkness and cannot answer."

In stark contrast to the pagan epitaphs, are the nearby Christian ones:

"Here lies Marcia, put to rest in a dream of peace."

"Lawrence to his sweetest son, borne away of angels."

"Victorious in peace and in Christ."

"Being called away, he went in peace."

This confidence in an infinitely better life after death and an actual looking forward to going home to be with Jesus caught the intrigue of many, many unbelievers, though for others it was a matter of disdain. A pagan philosopher of the day wrote, *"Only Christians and idiots are not afraid to die."*

However, I believe we often overestimate the role persecution played in the spread of Christianity. I like to put it like this: **Christians won the respect of the people by the way**

they died; but they won the hearts of the people by the way they lived. What I really believe won most of the converts was the radical, no strings attached, sacrificial good the early saints wowed their world with. Michael Green agrees. *"They made the grace of God credible by a society of love and mutual care which astonished the pagans and was recognized as something entirely new. It lent persuasiveness to their claim that the New Age had dawned in Christ."* Let's look at just a few examples:

The astonishing love and kindness Christians showed each other. As no other generation of Christians, they exemplified our Lord's words, *"A new commandment I give to you, that you love one another; as I have loved you, that you also love one another. By this all will know that you are My disciples, if you have love for one another,"* (Jn. 13:34-35.)

Justin Martyr described this love, *"We who used to value the acquisition of wealth and possessions more than anything else now bring what we have into a common fund and share it with anyone who needs it. We used to hate and destroy one another and refused to associate with people of another race or country. Now, because of Christ, we live together with such people and pray for our enemies."*

Clement wrote of the person who became a Christ-follower, *"He impoverishes himself out of love, so that he is certain he may never overlook a brother in need, especially if he knows he can bear poverty better than his brother. He likewise considers the pain of another as his own pain. And if he suffers any hardship because of having given out of his own poverty, he does not complain."*

Especially significant is what the pagan leaders said of this new cult that had invaded their society. Julian the apostate lamented that Christianity, *"has been specially advanced through the loving service rendered to strangers and through their care of the burial of the dead. It is a scandal that there is not a single Jew who is a beggar and that the [Christians] care not only for their own poor but for ours as well; while those who belong to us look in vain for the help we should render them."* In a word, he is saying why don't we love like these Christians? Lucian, the pagan satirist wrote, *"The earnestness with which the people of this religion help one another in their needs is incredible. They spare themselves nothing for this end. Their first lawgiver put it into their heads that they were all brethren."*

The unconditional, practical love Christians showed to all men. In a world often ravaged by disease and plagues, the Christians stayed in disease riddled places to take care of their sick while most others were fleeing for their own safety. But not only did they care for their own fellow believers, they also cared the sick of those outside the faith when very often these people's family members had left! **And they cared with no strings attached**. In other words, they didn't say, "If you become a Christ-follower, we'll take care of you." No, they simply cared for these fellow human beings as part of their love for Christ. This, I believe was huge in gaining the trust of the people of their day.

There were two great epidemics in the 160s and 250s which set the stage for believers to love in an extraordinarily surprising fashion. Concerning the second great plague, Dionysius writes of his fellow Christians:

"Most of our brother-Christians showed unbounded love and loyalty, never sparing themselves and thinking only of one another. Heedless of danger, they took charge of the sick, attending to their every need and ministering to them in Christ, and with them departed this life serenely happy; for they were infected by others with the disease, drawing on themselves the sickness of their neighbors and cheerfully accepting their pains. Many, in nursing and curing others, transferred their death to themselves and died in their stead. The best of our brothers lost their lives in this manner."

Do you see what he is saying? Many of the believers lost their own lives because they contracted the same diseases of the sick they were caring for! The sick included unbelievers. Now contrast this with his description of how the pagans responded to the same crisis:

"The heathen behaved in the very opposite way. At the first onset of the disease, they pushed the sufferers away and fled from their dearest, throwing them into the roads before they were dead and treated unburied corpses as dirt, hoping thereby to avert the spread and contagion of the fatal disease; but do what they might, they found it difficult to escape."

These early Christ-followers also distinguished themselves by the way they tangibly cared for orphans, widows, the elderly, and infirmed. Tertullian writes, *"It is our care of the helpless, our practice of loving kindness that brands us in the eyes of many of our opponents. 'Only look,' they say, 'look how they love one another!'"*

Again, this sacrificial kindness and loving care was offered with no strings attached. People were in no way neglected if they didn't choose to become Christ followers. That's why so many were allured into the faith rather than pressured or pushed. Tertullian described to the Roman magistrates the character of the early believers:

"Having refuted the charges laid against us, let me now show what we really are. We are a body knit together by one faith, one discipline and one hope. We meet together as a congregation, uniting together to offer prayer to God. We pray for the emperors and all in authority, for the welfare of the world, for peace and for the delay of the final end. We read our holy scriptures to nourish our faith, hope, steadfastness and good habits. We hear exhortations and rebukes. We take such judging very seriously—as befits those who believe they are in the sight of God—especially seriously when anyone sins so grievously we have to cut them off from our prayer, our congregation and all sacred things.

Our elders preside over us, obtaining that honor not by money, but by their established character. There is no buying and selling in the things of God. Though we have a fund, but not because people can buy religion. Once a month, anyone who wants to makes a small donation—but only he who is able and willing; there is no compulsion. It is not spent on feasts, but to support and bury poor people, to provide for orphans, the elderly old persons, victims of shipwreck and those in prison for their faith."

Their saving and raising of discarded infant girls. In the Roman world of that day, infanticide was not only permitted but actually encouraged. Especially when it came to baby girls. Often the newborn girl would simply be tossed out into the street to die from the elements. We have this tragic letter from the first century written by a pagan named Hilarion to his wife: "*Know* *that I am still in Alexandria.... I ask and beg you to take good care of our baby son, and as soon as I received payment I shall send it up to you. If you are delivered (before I come home), if it is a boy keep it, if a girl, discard it."*

Unbelievable. But this was the kind of world that the early church inhabited. How did they respond? They were the only people who went around looking for these discarded baby girls, brought them home, and raised them as their own. And if they needed help financially, the community of believers gladly pitched in!

Their radical commitment to moral purity. It is difficult for us to comprehend how decadent the culture of that day had become, especially in sexuality. Women slaves were expected to service the male members of the family as simply part of their job description. Brothels were found at every sporting event and in all the pagan temples. When Paul writes to the Thessalonians, *"For this is the will of God, your sanctification: that you should abstain from sexual immorality; that each of you should know how to possess his own vessel in sanctification and honor, not in passion of lust, like the Gentiles who do not know God," (*I Thess. 4:3-5), he is calling these believers out to a standard sexual purity unheard of in that day. Their resolute commitment to sex only being enjoyed within the confines of the marriage union, doubtlessly won the hearts of many pagan women.

Reckless Hospitality. It was difficult to find places to stay in the cities and villages of those days. Visitors were often hard pressed to find accommodations to spend the night in many places. This is where the early believers won the hearts and respect of their fellow countrymen. Not only did they share their homes with fellow believers, they did the same with unbelievers as well. Again, with no strings attached. They didn't require these pagan guests to become Christ-followers; they simply extended genuine hospitality to these travelers. Their hospitality verged on being reckless in that they were the go-to place for virtually anyone who couldn't find a place to stay.

Its appeal to women. This factor has not been adequately explored it seems to me. There is no question that women constituted the largest percentage of the early church by far. As one scholar put it, the early church was *"a church disproportionately populated by women."* Why would that be? We don't have to look very far to find the answer I believe. The surprise factor. Who was it that was looking out for the discarded female babies? The church. Where else would a woman of that day go to hear the astonishing command to men, "*Husbands, love your wife as Christ loved the church,*" followed by specifics of what that love looks like? The church. Where else would she go hear, "*In Christ there is neither…male nor female?*" Nowhere but the church. Where else would she go to hear that she and her husband were "*co-heirs of the grace of life?*" Again, the church. There were so, so many good reasons for a woman of that day to join in with this surprise movement. And this they did…in droves.

Surprising lives. They were a central factor in the astronomical growth of believers during the first three centuries. They were also part and parcel of the impact the Moravians had on their day. John Wesley went to visit the Moravian home base of Herrnhut. He was so impressed by what he saw that he wrote in his journal, *"I would gladly have spent my life here; but my Master calling me to labour in another part of his vineyard… O when shall this Christianity cover the earth, as the 'waters cover the sea?'"*

And they are just as vital for us today. Unfortunately, far too much evangelicalism today is well described by another word—predictable. Utterly predictable. People know what to expect and what they expect is anything but compelling. Stiff, rigid, rule keepers. Joylessly active saints whose greatest goals are to be doctrinally pure and to remain uncontaminated by the world. Anything but surprising. Ellen Glasgow described her father, a Presbyterian elder, as *"He was entirely unselfish, and in his long life he never committed a pleasure."*

But every now and then one runs across a story which reminds us how wonderfully surprising and life-transforming authentic Christianity can actually be. Real life episodes which reawaken us to the reality that Christianity is not a straight-jacket of rules and regulations, but the spontaneous, unrehearsed adventure of simply being like Christ. The real Christ…the radical Christ… the Christ of the scriptures and not the Christ of the steeple. The Christ Who went places those in the religious community would never frequent, made close friends of people the church considers too dangerous to hang around, and blindsided unsuspecting sinners with a completely irrational and relentless love. A love so surprising, so wholly unexpected, so irresistible, that they would never be the same. Dr. John White writes:

"All the Gospel accounts tell us that sinners flocked around Jesus. His love for God brought him into contact with all manner of men and women, none of whom seemed to find him an embarrassment. Nor did Jesus consider them an embarrassment to him. It was the religious hierarchy who had difficulty with Jesus. And frequently, his association with disreputable types was a particular source of criticism by religious groups."

Churches and religious people today do not make friends easily with people who are looked down on in society—jailbirds, prostitutes, drug addicts, drunks, thieves. This suggests that they may not be so near to God as they suppose. "Sinners" do not find churches attractive, so that sinners and would-be saints often keep to their respective ghettos.

However, there are refreshing exceptions to the rule. Tony Campolo, professor of sociology at Eastern College, tells the story of his visit to Honolulu for a Christian Conference. On his first night there, he awoke sometime after three (a six hour time difference had confused his sleep pattern) and left the hotel in search of a place to get something to eat. Eventually he found a tiny coffee shop, with one man behind the bar who served him coffee and a doughnut. Tony was the only customer until, quite suddenly, the coffee shop was filled with girls. Some sat at small tables, others at the counter near Tony. From their conversation he learned an astonishing amount about Honolulu's night life, for the girls were discussing their night's work and their male clients. These girls were prostitutes. He tells the story:

I overheard the woman sitting beside me say, "Tomorrow's my birthday. I'm going to be thirty-nine." Her "friend" responded in a nasty tone, "So what do you want from me? A birthday party? What do you want? Ya want me to get you a cake and sing 'Happy Birthday?'" "Come on!" said the woman sitting next to me. "Why do you have to be so mean? I was just telling you, that's all. Why do you have to put me down? I was just telling you it was my birthday. I don't want anything from you. I mean, why should you give me a birthday party? I've never had a birthday party in my whole life. Why should I have one now?" When I heard that, I made a decision. I sat and waited until the women had left. Then I called over the fat guy behind the counter and I asked him, "Do they come in here every night?"

"Yeah!" he answered. "The one right next to me, does she come here every night?" "Yeah," he said. "That's Agnes. Yeah, she comes in here every night. Why d'ya wanta know?" "Because I heard her say that tomorrow is her birthday," I told him. "What do you say you and I do something about that? What do you think about us throwing a birthday party for her right here tomorrow night?" A cute smile slowly crossed his chubby cheeks and he answered with measured delight, "That's great! " "Look." I told him, "if it's OK with you, I'll get back here tomorrow morning about 2:30 and decorate the place. I'll even get a birthday cake!" "No way," said Harry (that was his name.) "The birthday cake's my thing. I'll make the cake."

At 2:30 the next morning, I was back at the diner. I had picked up some crepe-paper decorations at the store and had made a sign out of big pieces of cardboard that read, "Happy Birthday, Agnes!" I decorated the diner from one end to the other. I had that diner looking good. The woman who did the cooking must have gotten the word out on the street, because by 3:15 every prostitute in Honolulu was in the place. It was wall-to-wall prostitutes...and me!

At 3:30 on the dot, the door of the diner swung open and in came Agnes and her friend. I had everybody ready (after all I was kind of the emcee of the affair) and when they came in we all screamed, "Happy birthday!" Never have I seen a person so flabbergasted...so stunned...so shaken. Her mouth fell open. Her legs seemed to buckle a bit. Her friend grabbed her arm to steady her. As she was led to sit on one of the stools along the counter we all sang "Happy Birthday" to her. As we came to the end of our singing with "happy birthday dear Agnes, happy birthday to you," her eyes moistened, when the birthday cake with all the candles on it was carried out, she lost it and just openly cried.

Harry gruffly mumbled, "Blow out the candles, Agnes! Come on! Blow out the candles! If you don't blow out the candles, I'm gonna hafta blow out the candles." And, after an endless few seconds, he did. Then he handed her a knife and told her, "Cut the cake, Agnes. Yo, Agnes, we all want some cake."

Agnes looked down at the cake. Then without taking her eyes off it, she slowly and softly said, "Look Harry, is it all right with you if I... I mean is it OK if I kind of... want I want to ask you is...is it OK if keep the cake a little while? I mean is it all right if we don't eat it right away?" Harry shrugged and answered, "Sure! It's OK If you want to keep the cake, keep the cake. Take it home if you want to." "Can I?" she asked. Then looking at me she said, "I live just down the street a couple of doors. I want to take the cake home, OK? I'll be right back. Honest!" She got off the stool picked up the cake, and, carrying it like it was the Holy Grail walked slowly toward the door.

As we all just stood there motionless, she left. When the door closed there was a stunned silence in the place. Not knowing what else to do, I broke the silence by saying, "What do you say we pray?"

Looking back on it now it seems more than strange for a sociologist to be leading a prayer meeting with a bunch of prostitutes in a diner in Honolulu at 3:30 in the morning. But then it just felt like the right thing to do. I prayed for Agnes...When I finished, Harry leaned over the counter and with a trace of hostility in his voice, he said "Hay! You never told me you were a preacher. What kind of church do you belong to?" In one of those moments when just the right words came, I answered, "I belong to a church that throws birthday parties for whores at 3:30 in the morning." Harry waited a moment and then almost sneered as he answered, "No you don't. There's no church like that. If there was, I'd join it. I'd join a church like that!"

Astonishing! "I'd join a church like that." And perhaps if he found a church like that He would give himself to a Savior like that. Oh beloved, it matters that our Christianity be surprising. Warmly surprising. Unconditionally surprising. Jesus-like surprising. Let's not settle for anything less. The early saints didn't. The Moravians didn't. Now it's our turn...

Epilogue

Enemy-occupied territory—that is what this world is. Christianity is the story of how the rightful king has landed; you might say landed in disguise, and is calling us to take part in a great campaign of sabotage.
—C.S. Lewis

WE HAVE NOW CONCLUDED OUR look at the "original game plan" that we spoke of in the Introduction. A game plan that is badly in need of resurrection, and yet one that offers untold hope and stunning possibilities for the Kingdom radicals of today. There is absolutely no reason that this epic past couldn't become our blueprint for a far preferable future than the one we seem to be heading in.

If one of the saints of the early church were able to visit the Christian landscape of today, what words of advice might he or she have for us? Among the many things I'm sure he or she would have to say, let me suggest that these four would be somewhere at the top of the list. I imagine they would say something to this effect:

Be sure to keep your first Love, your first love.

The single most important reason for the impact we had in our day was the all-consuming, ever-deepening love affair we had with a Person. A Person named Jesus. He was everything to us.

We couldn't get enough of Him. It was He and He alone Who provided a blatantly supernatural peace that enabled us to move forward in a world that was tearing in on us from almost every direction. His joy sustained us when all shreds of human happiness were taken from us. His love was the feast and delight of our souls, particularly when our families and friends turned their backs on us. Frankly, we never got over the magic, the mystery, and the wonder of this Man from Galilee Who absolutely turned our worlds upside down. We went to every length possible to take the time to simply sit at His feet, listen to His voice, pour our hearts out to Him, and simply relish His exquisite beauty. We were worshippers far before we were anything else.

You Christians today are too busy. So busy trying to serve the Lord that you don't have time to simply enjoy Him. In fact, for many of you the idea of enjoying God is a foreign concept. You're trying to serve God, to obey God, to be faithful to God, to know more about God, etc. But the thought of simply spending quiet, unhurried, extended time alone with God for no other purpose than simply to enjoy Him seems—well, let's be honest—a bit of a waste of time. Oh my friends, nothing could be further from the truth!

Too often your greatest passion is for a *cause* rather than a *Person.* You're more concerned with effectively serving God than deeply knowing God. We understand that; we struggled at times with the very same thing. Martha (Lk. 10:38-42) and our fellow believers in Ephesus (Rev. 2:1-7) all fell into that same trap. But let me encourage you once again, keep close to Jesus. A close, intimate walk with Jesus has to be fought for; it never simply falls into place.

Be a Mary: *"And she had a sister called Mary, who also sat at Jesus' feet and heard His word,"* (Lk. 10:39.)

Be a David: *"One thing I have desired of the Lord, that will I seek: that I may dwell in the house of the Lord all the days of my life, to behold the beauty of the Lord, and to inquire in His temple,"* (Ps. 27:4.)

Be a Paul: *"Yet indeed I also count all things loss for the excellence of the knowledge of Christ Jesus my Lord, for whom I have suffered the loss of all things, and count them as rubbish, that I may gain Christ, thatand the fellowship of His sufferings, being conformed to His death, if, by any means, I may attain to the resurrection from the dead,"* (Phil. 3:8-11.)

Be a fanatic about keeping your roots deep. Everything, but everything, of true spiritual consequence flows from that fountain. But remember, deep roots don't just happen. They are cultivated at the expense of by-passing many other pressing things. Often good things. But not good enough things.

Spend more time with non-Christians. Far more time.

I know this may sound strange, but many of you are spending too much time with fellow Christians. And some of you are spending *way* too much time. Now I realize of course, that some of you are not spending enough time with other believers and that is an even greater problem.

We reached the unbelievers of our day primarily through one simple strategy. We very purposefully befriended those whom

God brought into our path or were part of our natural sphere of influence. We spent time with them, got to know them, ate meals and drank wine with them, went to varying cultural events with them, etc.

We took very seriously our Lord's example that he was a "*friend*" of tax collectors and sinners. Not an acquaintance, but a friend. And there is no way to become a friend without spending time with them. We found that as we laid this foundation of friendship, sharing what Jesus meant to us was very natural for the most part. In fact, very often *they* were the ones initiating the conversation as to our faith and why we were so different.

It seems to me that you believers today are seeking to win converts primarily through *events* and *programs*. You hold evangelistic rallies, Christian concerts, and develop church programs that send people out to share their faith with whoever will listen. And let me say, I love that you are at least trying to reach out to unbelievers. Too often the church has retreated from even trying to reach the lost.

But your approach doesn't feel natural much of the time. I can't help but think that many of the people you are trying to reach must feel like they are a project more than a person. What worked so effectively for us is that we reached out to our unbelieving friends and neighbors first and foremost as fellow human beings. We always sought to maintain the attitude that we were simply "one beggar telling other beggars where we found bread." We sought ways to bless them with no strings attached. After a while they usually got curious about why we treated them the way we did and we were able to share very naturally and spontaneously the *"reason for the hope"* within us, (I Pet. 3:15.)

You also have a commodity at your disposal which never existed for us. You have *church buildings*. We never knew such a thing as we almost always met in secret or at someone's home. I don't think there is anything inherently wrong with having such a structure. But I have noticed two things which concern me.

First, it seems to me that too often an inordinate amount of time, money, and energy is being spent on these structures which God has promised that He will burn out of existence one day, (II Pet. 3:10.) The structures God has called us to be laser focused upon are made of human flesh and house eternal souls. Now clearly there is nothing wrong with having a nice facility to meet and worship in. So I am not advocating getting rid of these structures. However, it seems to me that the danger arises when the constructing and maintaining of these buildings is drawing away precious time, money, and energy from the battle that matters most—namely the Great Commission. Christ never said, "Go you therefore and build buildings among all the nations," but rather, "Go you therefore and make disciples of all the nations," (Mtt. 28:18-20.) Nothing makes the gospel an issue more than supernaturally-changed lives. As long as your church buildings serve as a tool in seeing this happen, then they justify their existence.

Secondly, while many good and godly things are clearly taking place within the confines of your church buildings, one thing vitally concerns me. So many of you Christians have made the building a sort of refuge from this evil world. It is your safe harbor from the ills of this world and your almost exclusive "third place" outside of work and the home. This why I say that many of you are spending too much time with fellow believers.

We loved our times of getting together for worship, bible study, and prayer. They were precious and so important for our personal spiritual growth. But those times never took the place of often even more time spent moving out into the waters where the fish naturally congregate. We saw fellowship with other believers as a wonderful and necessary preparation for significantly impacting unbelievers, but never as a replacement for the adventure and high calling of doing hand to hand combat with the prince of darkness for the souls of lost men and women.

Specialize in surprise.

I say this as kindly as I know how, but you evangelicals today are...how do I say it...too predictable. Of course, there are wonderful exceptions to this. The stunning response that many of the Amish saints made to the tragic killings in their schoolroom in 2006 was a fantastic example of this. Well done!

I think one of the very main reasons we were able to penetrate the world of our day was our God-empowered resolve to bless the people of our day, no strings attached. In other words we never said, "Now if you become a Christ-follower, we will do this or that for you." Rather we simply followed the lead of our God Who *"makes His sun rise on the evil and on the good, and sends rain on the just and on the unjust,"* (Mtt. 5:43-48.) I believe that what really gained the curiosity of the unbelievers around us were the random, unrehearsed, reckless acts of kindness and tangible good that we freely heaped upon them, even our enemies. No, especially our enemies. People couldn't figure us out. Emperors couldn't figure us out. But as we quietly went about doing good, bringing home infant girls left to die in the street, caring for the sick whether they were Christ-followers or not, providing warm hospitality to almost anyone in need (false teachers were our primary exception), the hearts of the pagans began to soften toward our cult. And many, many of them became Christ-followers because the surprise factor in our lives won us the right to be heard.

Simply put, we led by surprise. Which were exactly the marching orders our Savior gave us in His Kingdom Manifesto—the Sermon on the Mount, (Mtt.5-7.) As one reads the words in that sermon, they are stained by the word "surprise" from beginning to end. We took those words seriously, very seriously.

The last thing I would say along these same lines is this. Too often you are more passionate about what you are against than what you are for. Or to put it another way, there is a great need in your day for men and women to speak with greater passion about what is right with Christ than what is wrong with the world. We never tried to change Rome. We simply sought to spotlight our dear Savior through our lives and our lips. Our greatest agenda was not to change culture but to at least temporarily disrupt people's light view of God, and especially His Christ. Our primary message was not the ills of Roman society (of which there were many), but the breathtaking stunning-ness of Jesus. We found that there is an unmistakably unique power in laser focusing upon Christ, in extolling His unfathomable beauties, in relaying His life-transforming word, and in simply remaining hidden in His shadow. In the final analysis, the most surprising Person Who ever walked this planet was this Galilean carpenter turned Rabbi turned Savior. We just tried as best we could to let others in on the surprise. May God grant that you all are able to do the same.

Make discipleship the business of all God's people.

Without a doubt, one of the most important and dynamic features of the influence we exerted in our day was our "all hands on deck" approach to spiritual mentoring and discipleship. We saw it as absolutely normative for *every* believer to pass on to other believers what they knew of God and the Christian life. As we passed these vitals truths on, we did so with the expectation that our mentees would turn around and do the same thing. We understood that truth was not to be *transferred* from one saint to another but *entrusted*. Which is exactly what Paul taught us: *"And the things that you have heard from me among many witnesses, commit these to faithful men who will be able to teach others also,"* (II Tim. 2:2.)

We never had bible studies just for bible studies sake. Our times together in the word of God felt more like the passing out of ammunition than the learning of new doctrines. Certainly we wholeheartedly believed in the importance of learning doctrine, and of going deeper and deeper in the word. But it was because we knew that each day we were walking into a hostile world and that the truths we learned would be vital in strengthening and sustaining our encroachments upon Satan's territory. We also were convinced to the core of our being that we had nothing more important or more powerful to offer our fellow man than the living, breathing, life-transforming word of God.

We specialized in discipling and mentoring those people who were in our own natural web of connectedness. In other words, Roman soldiers discipled fellow Roman soldiers, elite ladies mentored other elite ladies, slaves influenced other slaves, etc. To tell you the truth, it was magic. It spread like wildfire. The natural connection we had with others in our own unique sphere of influence provided the perfect bridge for the word of God to march over unimpeded into waiting lives. Then these recipients became so excited about what they were learning that they immediately began looking for others to pass these truths along to. Like the earliest disciples, most of us *"were not able to not speak the things"* we had seen and heard, (Acts 4:20.)

For us, discipleship never felt like a program or a spiritual obligation. Certainly we knew that it was a central command from our Lord (Mtt. 28:18-20), but it seemed more like a new instinct, a sort of inward restlessness that would not be put to bed until we found someone we could help shape and mold for Kingdom purposes.

One of the things that most concerns me about discipleship in your day is that it is no longer "all hands on deck." And it hasn't been for a very long time, unfortunately. The work of passing along the word of God has been reserved almost exclusively for those who are considered professionals in the church world (as if there ever was such a thing as a professional Christian.) Those who have attended a special school, have received specialized training, and have been awarded a specialized honor called "ordination," are now front and center in the process of discipleship. They are seen as the "professionals", which obviously means that everyone else is an "amateur." The term I believe you people use is "clergy vs. laity."

Candidly, this makes me want to pull my hair out. Now I recognize that you were born into this system which has been going on for more than 1500 years, so I am careful to not fault you too severely. But I fault with every fiber of my being this system. It is a direct contradiction to the doctrine we held as so precious—the priesthood of all believers. You see, most of us were converted out of systems which held strongly to a clergy/laity distinction. Whether we were Jews or worshipped the Roman gods, each had its own temple and temple priests who had special access to their deity. For us to hear the words that all of us—no exception—were "*a chosen generation, a royal priesthood, a holy nation*," (I Pet. 2:9) was a thrill beyond description and provided a humble dignity our souls relished on a daily basis. **It also reminded us that all of God's people are in "full time" ministry.** Our *occupations* varied—soldier, tent maker, pottery maker, etc.—but we all had the very same *vocation*. Our number one calling in life was to be an out and out, no holds barred, disciple of Jesus Christ. As I said before, everyone had a vital part to play in this greatest of all sieges and we never saw some Christians as clergy and others as lay people. Yes, we had leaders in our churches but never professionals.

The position of "senior pastor" never existed for the first 300 years. We always had a plurality of leaders—elders, deacons/deaconesses but never one single individual who became the premier teacher, shepherd, and vision-caster for the church. Gifted older men and women shared the teaching and shepherding responsibilities while everyone else was either being discipled or making disciples. Usually it was both. And, as I said, it worked like magic.

The danger of paid professionals doing all the work is beautifully described by one of your own people—John Stott. He writes:

"What model of the church, then should we keep in our minds? The traditional model is that of the pyramid, with the pastor perched precariously on its pinnacle, like a little pope in his own church, while the laity are arrayed beneath him in serried ranks of inferiority. Not much better is the bus image, with the pastor as driver and the laity as passive passengers being taken to a pastorally appointed destination. It is a totally unbiblical image, because the New Testament envisages not a single pastor with a docile flock but both a plural oversight...and an every member ministry."

I will say though, I am very encouraged by clear evidence in recent years that more and more of your people are hungering to return to this "all hands on deck" model which worked so powerfully in our day. Even more and more senior pastors and church staff are coming back to the original game plan. They are seeing their primary ministry as one of equipping the people in the pew to be more effective game changers within and outside the church. They are experiencing the joy and deep satisfaction of broadly decentralized ministry. I thank God for each of them. Risky as it seems at times, few things will make your churches more dangerous to Satan's kingdom than putting ministry back into the hands of those to whom it actually and biblically belongs—all of God's people. May God bless you mightily in coming days!

And so my dear brothers and sisters, know that we are watching you from above, cheering wildly for your every effort to glorify our Father and make Christ known to the people of your day. We've run our race, made our mistakes, and enjoyed God's successes through us. But now "the night has come when no man can work." (Jn. 9:4.)

Now it's your turn. This is your day, your time, your season, and your opportunity to "work the works of Him Who sent you while it is day." As we used to say—*carpe diem.* "Seize the day," my friends, you'll never have another chance. Seize it through being gate crashers and game changers. Seize it by taking to heart the words of Paul:

"Finally, my brethren, be strong in the Lord and in the power of His might. Put on the whole armor of God, that you may be able to stand against the wiles of the devil. For we do not wrestle against flesh and blood, but against principalities, against powers, against the rulers of the darkness of this age, against spiritual hosts of wickedness in the heavenly places. Therefore take up the whole armor of God, that you may be able to withstand in the evil day, and having done all, to stand.

Stand therefore, having girded your waist with truth, having put on the breastplate of righteousness, and having shod your feet with the preparation of the gospel of peace; above all, taking the shield of faith with which you will be able to quench all the fiery darts of the wicked one. And take the helmet of salvation, and the sword of the Spirit, which is the word of God; praying always with all prayer and supplication in the Spirit, being watchful to this end with all perseverance and supplication for all the saints." Eph. 6:10-18

I can't give you any better advice. You are in the midst of a cosmic warfare that requires you to know and appropriate every single resource God has provided you. We could never, ever have faced the things we did, endured the fiery trials which came our way, responded so surprisingly to our enemies, if it hadn't been for resurrection power backing us every step of the way. What was available and so necessary for us, is every bit as much your birthright. So I plead with you – "Put on the full armor of God." Then go out into the world and play your God-scripted part to the hilt. Do this and you will find at the end of your earthly sojourn that God has made you and used you to be game changers. Eternal game changers. And you will have spent your few days on earth trafficking in the most titanically high use of any person's life – game changing Christianity.

About the Author - Dwight Edwards

Dwight is the fifth great grandson of renowned theologian and pastor, Jonathan Edwards. He has pastored for over thirty years in various capacities. He ministered for 23 years at Grace Bible Church in College Station, TX. From 1980-1990 he served as the college pastor and from 1990-2003 he ministered as the senior pastor of the 2500 member congregation. He presently serves as the teaching pastor of WatersEdge Community Church in Houston,Tx. and the High Performance Coach at River Oaks Country Club. He is also the founder of Club Impact Ministries – an outreach dedicated to "Bringing Christ Into Unexpected Arenas."

Dwight is a bestselling author and has written six previous books – *Revolution Within, Releasing the Rivers Within, A Tale of Three Ships, Kindling for the Fire, Say 'No' to Vanilla,* and *High Octane for the Spirit.* He also has a workbook entitled *Experiencing Christ Within* and has written numerous magazine articles.

A former professional tennis player, he has ministered throughout the United States and many places in the world over the last 30 years. He is also widely sought after as a motivational speaker for businesses, schools, athletic teams, and governmental agencies. He has given presentations at Yale, Princeton, The Air Force Academy, Vanderbilt, Rice, Texas A&M University, and many other schools. He is a graduate of The University of Mary Hardin Baylor and attended Dallas Theological Seminary. Dwight and his wife Lauri live in Houston.

Links:
www.clubimpactministries.com
www.revolutionwithin.com
www.watersedgehouston.org
www.highoctaneforthemind.com
www.toolboxlunches.com